Black Heart Life

CHRISTINA CRIDEBRING

This is a true story of my lived experience. This book was written by memory and mine is imperfect. I've done my best to be faithful to my experiences and emotions as I remember them. In order to maintain the anonymity of the innocent (and the guilty), in some instances I have changed the names of individuals or places, the details of events, identifying characteristics, occupations or places of residence.

Copyright © 2024 by Black Heart Life, LLC

All rights reserved. No part of this book may be reproduced or used in any manner without written permission of the copyright owner except for the use of quotations in a book review. For more information, address: blackheartlifebook@gmail.com.

First paperback edition October 29, 2024

Book cover design by Kamar Martin

ISBN # 979-8-9913674-0-0 (paperback)
ISBN # 979-8-9913674-2-4 (ebook)
ISBN # 979-8-9913674-1-7 (hardcover)

www.christinacridebring.com

SSG

I'm glad to see you turned out fairly normal despite my parenting and you've made none of the relationship mistakes I did. Love you! ♥

Contents

Chapter 1: Welcome to My Shit Show 1

Chapter 2: Adios Bitchachos 59

Chapter 3: Home for the Holidays 139

Chapter 4: Here I Go Again 151

Chapter 5: Now What? 239

Chapter 6: The Last Act 251

Chapter 7: Afterword 269

About the Author 273

CHAPTER 1

Welcome to My Shit Show

It was hard to believe I was on a plane, bound for places I'd only dreamed about, packed for unknown adventures that miraculously fit into a single suitcase. A year earlier, I would have never seen this turn of events coming in my life. At that point, I was five years into a long-term relationship and was quite content living my regular, ordinary life. Back then, traveling was only something we did when we could tear ourselves away from work for a quick vacation, which was almost never. My boyfriend, Tom, had one of the top operational leadership roles with a start-up company that experienced record growth and had recently been bought out by a much larger company. While he had the freedom to go on vacation, he was constantly taking calls and putting out work-related fires. That didn't bother me because his company held a special place in my heart. I had previously worked for that same company but had left after meeting Tom. We had met through work, and a lot of our close friends were former colleagues of mine or current colleagues of Toms. In fact, we had recently returned from one of our elusive vacations a few months before, where we bought into a beautiful golf villa timeshare in Mexico with one of our good friends, who was also a vendor for Tom's company. It may seem a little too friendly to constantly be surrounded by 'work-people', but I'd always found great friendships in the workplace. So I had no qualms about our commitment to spending one week a year in Mexico with 'work-people.'

Plus, I had always adored Mexico. My fascination with Latin cultures started in childhood, though I can't trace it back to a specific event or reason. Latin culture and language fascinated me for most of my life. Don't get me wrong, this fascination never inspired a strong grasp of the language. I could still only manage to butcher very common phrases in my white-girl Spanglish, "Donde esta el bano?" or "Dos cervezas, por favor." Despite my lack of fluency, my travel bucket list consisted of three Latin countries: Spain, Peru, and Cuba.

I had *always* wanted to go to Spain. Maybe because my dad got me a computer game back in the day when games were programmed on big floppy disks inserted into your computer, which was a whole separate unit from your monitor. I'd spend hours hunting treasures throughout all the major cities in Spain using clues in Espanol and typing commands like, 'Go to the bullfighting ring in Madrid.' Yes, he was one of *those* dads who thought I should be studying even when I was playing games. Spoiler alert: I also grew up to be *that* mom.

Peru, because I saw an episode of *Extreme Makeover: Weight Loss Edition* where Chris Powell took a participant to Machu Picchu as their mid-challenge reward for losing some ridiculous amount of weight. Watching the footage of beautiful Incan ruins high in the mountains and surrounded by lush, tropical vegetation, I immediately knew I had to go see it for myself! I remember searching for a photo of Machu Picchu and setting it as my background photo on Facebook because I wanted to be reminded of the beauty every day.

And Cuba, because I felt compelled to go see it before all the white people destroyed it! Yes, a white girl just said that 'white people' would destroy it. In case you weren't aware, my race has a reputation for destroying culture and introducing disgusting levels of consumerism in those places we adopt as our tourist hot spots.

When I was in high school, I thought I'd develop the courage to study abroad in Spain by the time I went off to college. By college, I had developed no such courage and couldn't even imagine the possibility of leaving the state to go to school. I'd never existed a single day without the security of my family and friends at home. I'd never been particularly outgoing, so the idea of traveling somewhere alone, talking to strangers, and having to make all new friends was too big a leap out of my comfort zone. By the time I was twenty-one, I was pregnant with my beautiful daughter Sage, and any ideas of traveling were replaced with concerns about daycare, formula and diapers. When I finally started earning enough to afford more than only diapers and food, I never felt stable enough to even plan consistent vacations, much less expensive trips abroad. My travel bucket list fizzled away into the mundane of my daily life, and I never thought much about it unless I was reflecting on the good ol' days and things I'd never accomplished.

While I never wanted to re-marry after my divorce, I still always found myself in a serious relationship. This point in time was no exception. I had found myself a nice man, Tom, and settled down into the same life that married couples experience, minus the piece of paper signed by a government representative. We were happy, although it wasn't in a fireworks show kind of way. But I was okay with that. It was like your favorite pair of pants that always fit when you put them on. They may not be entirely flattering, a little out of style, and the knees are worn, but they fit every time. It was predictable. There was no drama, no fighting, and the most important thing to me was he treated me well. I lived with a lot of autonomy, which is exactly how I liked things.

In fact, Tom had recently purchased a new home and had given me complete control over the remodel. As much as I tried to involve him in the decisions, he would defer to my judgment. I actually wanted his final sign-off—it was his money, after all— and this remodel wasn't cheap. I didn't want him to be mad or hate it.

But Tom never got mad and never hated anything or anyone. So, I happily chose everything, from baseboards and countertops to light fixtures and crown molding. (Getting to be in charge is my favorite!) And believe me, when I tell you that I *loved* the process of seeing my visions become reality. I'd visualize how the backsplash would complement the tile or the reclaimed wood would make the kitchen island pop. In no time, the final result appeared before my eyes. Honestly, this project was the most fun I had in a long time. It was the first year we were empty nesters, as his son and my daughter had both moved out recently, and this was the house we planned to live in for years to come. It was almost complete after a month of contractors working day and night. My organizational skills and directness guided the project to completion—in what I was told—record time. I wanted to tackle a few small projects myself, so I took the next several months to complete the more minor details. I was still contemplating curtain options when my world was blown to shit.

Breaking Up

Tom was a pretty ordinary guy, in a nerdy IT guy kind of way (no offense, IT guys). He wasn't ugly but wasn't knock-your-socks-off handsome either. With clothes on, you might imagine he was athletic when, in actuality, he had the Dad bod of a Mountain Dew-drinking, video gaming, IT guy. He would easily blend into any corporate conference room. So then, "*What were you attracted to?*" you might be thinking. After a long streak of dating the wrong men, which technically started in high school, I had set an intention to finally find a *nice* man. As you got to know Tom, his positivity and sense of humor would win you over. He had the ability to make you feel like everything was going to be okay. And he was *soooo* attentive. He made me feel like I was the only person in the room, even if we were in a room full of beauty queens. Not that we ever were in a room full of beauty queens, but you know what I mean…he *never* looked at other women.

Tom's salary and his generous nature afforded me the opportunity to not need to work. He was the first man I ever allowed myself to rely on financially. While I had been married previously, I had always worked and kept my finances separate. Volunteering at a pit bull rescue was my only 'job' at that point, as I had left my former career in the human resources and recruiting space. I obtained my real estate license, and we had some money carved out for me to start flipping homes once our remodel was complete. A few weeks prior, Tom had been relieved of his position, but I still wasn't too worried, as he had received an excellent severance package and had transferrable skills and a great attitude. It wouldn't be long before he was back at it for a new company.

One morning, I was volunteering at the pit bull rescue, sitting out in the exercise yard with one of the dogs, when I got a call from someone I used to work with. Several years prior, I had been your average corporate recruiter when a colleague had given me a chance to work in a high-volume, results-oriented environment. I loved that adrenaline and the satisfaction of putting processes in place that allowed us to crush our goals. It had been years since I had spoken with him, so even though I typically don't answer my phone, I decided to take his call. One of the executives we used to work for had a new project, and they needed someone with my background to help out. It piqued my interest, so I asked him to set up a meeting so I could learn more. I was supposed to be retired from the recruitment business. My days consisted of going to CrossFit, overseeing the remodel of the house, and volunteering with abused pit bulls. Would it be worth giving up that freedom? I was willing to at least have a discussion around it.

A few days later, I was quickly entranced with their idea to create a boutique recruitment agency that would help support the students in their software development boot camp. What do I know about coding or developers? Nada. Maybe Tom could help me get up to speed since he was well-versed in the IT industry. If nothing else, I had confidence in my ability to learn new things, so I was all in. It's so weird how, a week prior, this idea would have never crossed my mind, yet here I was, coming up with a general outline of a business plan.

Fortunately for me, I had a good friend who ran a large division for a successful recruitment agency.

Ironically, her company also supported recruitment for Tom's company, so we all became fast friends, and she was the same one we had vacationed with in Mexico a few months prior. Tom had even bought into their amazing beach villa timeshare on the golf course so that we could return each year. I reached out to her in the hopes that she would tell me if she thought my business plan was realistic, so I didn't lead these investors down a dead-end path. Luckily, she agreed to review my plan and provide feedback at happy hour the next day.

My business plan was simply a short outline of all my general ideas, so it didn't take long to review and discuss a few areas that needed tweaking. But I was happy to learn that my instincts were pretty in line with her experience. With that out of the way, we could enjoy our drinks and catch up. My mind wandered for a minute as I wondered when the last time I saw her was. Even though we'd just seen each other during our trip to Mexico two months ago, I realized I hadn't seen her since. I sucked at making plans, so I made a mental note to plan another happy hour with the guys before we finished with our meeting.

We settled into catching up, and something felt... strained. A few moments ago, when we were talking about business, the conversation was flowing naturally, and nothing seemed out of the ordinary. Oddly, once we moved to personal conversation I saw a quizzical look pass over her face when I mentioned something about Tom. I kept moving on in the conversation without much thought except maybe she had gas? But she seemed a little on edge just shooting the shit, which wasn't like her. She seemed like she was trying to evaluate something, but I was the hyper-analytic one who was always analyzing. She was typically bubbly and outgoing. The conversation moved on to upcoming plans for the summer, and as I mentioned something Tom and I planned to do, she blurted out, "*Are you still with him?*" in a perplexed tone. Genuine confusion was on her face this time, which couldn't be at all mistaken for holding in gas.

Now, I was the one who was confused. "Why wouldn't I still be with him?" I asked in surprise. It popped into my head that maybe she thought I was some sort of gold digger who would have dumped Tom when he lost his job. But that didn't make sense because when we started dating, I was making more money than him.

"You really don't know?!" she almost whispered to herself. Thinking my assumption was correct, I replied, "Of course, I know he lost his job, but why would I dump him for that?" I could tell this subject was making her incredibly uncomfortable, and she was unsure how to respond. "Do you know why he lost his job?" she asked. By this point, I was overly confused. Why wouldn't I know? I quickly relayed the reasoning he had given me, thinking back to the day he had told me.

Her jaw hung open, and I think she only breathed the quizzical word, "Whaaaat?" Immediately, she excused herself from the table for the restroom, leaving me to sit there wondering what the hell was going on.

When she returned, she offered, "I don't think you have the full story on Tom's exit from the company" She apologized and said she couldn't say anything more due to her relationship with Tom's company. She made it clear that she shouldn't even be talking to me, but she had wanted to help me with the business plan. "I'm sorry, I thought you had left him, which is why you were job hunting. I agreed to meet today because I was trying to help you out so that you could get back on your feet. I know you quit your job last year," she said. I was dumbfounded. Not talking to *me*....why?

"So, you aren't going to talk to me ever again?" I asked, bewildered.

"I'm sorry, it really has nothing to do with you. Given the nature of my business, I need to distance myself for a while." She reassured me that she was still my friend and was rooting for me to figure it all out, but she couldn't be part of it. She was practically squirming to get out of the restaurant, and I almost felt bad for her, as she was clearly conflicted about whatever she knew that I didn't. If she wasn't supposed to be talking to me, it meant I couldn't ask her questions or anyone else in our colleague circle who had a connection to Tom's company. She at least confirmed that they were no longer friends with Tom and were planning to buy out his portion of their timeshare that he had bought into a few months prior.

What in the actual fuck?! So Tom was aware of whatever was going on. What was causing my friend to act so weird, to cut me off, to be there offering to help me go back to work only because she thought Tom and I had split? What could have made Tom lie about his separation from the company and job he loved? What would have caused our friends to buy back our portion of the timeshare? And why had they had cut him off? Cut us both off, technically. Only he knew about it and knew why, but he didn't tell me. Why did she think that I had left him? Whatever she knew would have to be a pretty big *something*. The surprised tone of her voice when she uttered the question, "Are you still with *him*?" stuck with me and replayed in my mind. Why wouldn't I still be with him?

For the last five years, I had 100% thought I was finally dating the nice guy. But something about her question, *"Are you still with him?"* told me everything I needed to know without telling me anything at all. He had done something and it was bad enough that the people who knew about it thought I had left him. The sinking in my stomach didn't even feel real. There was a ringing in my ears, and I felt confused, disoriented. Walking into this meeting, I had already thought I was about to turn my life upside down, but in a positive way, for a new career opportunity. This news blindsided me like a wave wiping you out in the ocean for the first time. The water hits you hard and knocks you down under the surface. You think you'll pop back up to the surface, like in a swimming pool, but there's a current underneath pulling you round and round. Water is up your nose, and you're choking, trying to figure out which way is up. Once your body floats back to the top and your head breaks the surface, another wave splashes your face, and you choke and sputter, gasping for breath with a desperation so real.

How could this be happening?

Just breathe, I reminded myself as I started to panic. This wave wasn't real water; it was a metaphorical emotional wave hitting me square in the face.

What could have happened at work that would have caused people to cut bait with Tom? Did he steal? It was possible, but it would have to be some serious embezzlement for a vendor to have learned about it. Did he murder someone? Were there actual skeletons in his closet? No, he would have been arrested for that. What could he have done that would cause our friends to disown him?

While my friend gave me no clues to work with, my gut was telling me that he cheated. That *had* to be it. Even though it didn't make sense why my friend would know about his infidelity or what that had to do with work, my instinct couldn't move away from this hypothesis.

What in the hell was I going to do? How could this be happening to me *again*? Tom was a nice guy; he didn't do things like this. That was why I picked him, so I never had to feel deceived again. It had happened with so many before him you would think I'd be used to it by now. But somehow, this was worse because I didn't suspect I was being deceived. There were no nights that I waited up for him to come home from a night of unabated drinking. Hell, he doesn't ever drink more than one or two beers. There were no work trips to slip away unnoticed with a secret lover. There were no jealous quarrels over shady phone calls or longing glances at another woman. Everything was exactly how a good relationship was supposed to be. Or so I thought.

We lived together for five years. We shared a life. What was I supposed to do? Where was I supposed to go, to live? What about all our plans?

Breathe.

My life was spiraling out of my control, but I didn't even know exactly how, what, or especially…why? Deep down, I knew that my familiar life was over. My gut and heart knew something, but the details were something my brain hadn't figured out yet.

Most would expect to hear next that I flew into a rage, confronted him, and drama ensued. That would have been a normal and somewhat justified response. But sadly, this was not my first (or even my second or third) experience with assholes who lied or cheated. Perhaps this magnitude of deception was novel, though. I don't think I had ever met a true sociopath before, but I had seen my fair share of liars. The thing about liars is…*they lie*. So, confronting a liar about *why* they lied is a very untherapeutic experience. Predictably, they lie more about their previous lies in order to string you along, thus wasting even more precious minutes of your life.

Not today, Satan.

Tom was going to be leaving for an annual fishing trip in two days, and I looked forward to these trips each year. Not because I went with him but because I stayed home and got to have the house to myself. Since I have always been a committed neat freak, and Tom and the kids weren't, it was my opportunity to clean the house and live alone in a clean and tidy abode for one whole week a year. You're probably thinking that I'm the crazy one now, which is somewhat true when it comes to a neat and orderly home. I've been called a nazi once or twice (don't get your panties in a bunch, they were using the term as slang to describe someone controlling). Though I am an uber-efficient partially German girl who loves to clean and organize. Everything has its place, and that brings me soothing comfort, like a blankie for a toddler.

By this point, all the kids had moved out, but when they were home, not a damn person in the house was tidy besides me. Tom's son was the oldest. He was 21 and living with his girlfriend. My daughter, Sage, was the next oldest. She was entering her final year of college and moved in with her boyfriend the week prior. When she moved out this time, it wasn't only for the school year. I knew that she would never live at home again and that I was truly an empty nester. She had been dating her boyfriend since she was sixteen, and it felt permanent when they moved in together. It was a bittersweet feeling as a mother. While on one hand, I knew I would miss Sunday evenings spent in the loft watching the Kardashians; I was also incredibly proud of how mature and focused Sage and her boyfriend were. Tom's daughter was the youngest, and she lived with her mom. She never particularly enjoyed visiting our house anyway, so we were officially alone.

Initially, I looked forward to the upcoming fishing trip in anticipation of spending the first day of Tom's absence cleaning, and the next six days in quiet bliss. But my excitement to clean was cast aside when I learned the truth about Tom. Instead, I would be using that week to pack my belongings and move out.

Here is the catch...you knew there had to be one coming. *Tom didn't know that I knew.* I didn't confront him after my insane happy hour and ensuing state of confusion. Instead, I acted as normal as possible, knowing that in a couple of days I would have the house to myself so I could think. (Maybe that makes me a little bit of a sociopath myself.) For the next two days, my gym sessions suddenly took me hours during the day, and I over-scheduled my evenings full of plans with friends to keep me out of the house so I didn't have to fake pleasant conversation. I'm not much of an actress and I couldn't look at him the same way. The clear blue eyes that I used to think looked so kind and thoughtful, suddenly appeared calculating and cold. My internal timer was counting down to Saturday morning when his flight would take off and send him to a lake in Canada.

After driving him to the airport, I could finally take a deep inhale and exhale into the stupor that would be my life for a bit. Before I could go home, I had an appointment to meet a friend at the gym. Besides needing to lift some weights, I also needed to ask a question. This particular friend had caught their fiancé cheating by secretly installing spyware on their computer following some suspicious behavior. After a brief explanation of my situation, I asked for the name of the spyware, as I had every intention of going home to hack Tom's computer, access all our phone records, and turn the house upside down until I found whatever clues I could to answer the million questions in my mind. My friend had some insightful words that changed my whole course of action and made things crystal clear for the first time in days. He said, "It sounds like you have already made up your mind to leave Tom. You want spyware to figure out why you are leaving, but you are already planning your exit. If that's the case, you may not want to go through this process. Anything you find using spyware, you can *never* go back in time and *unsee* it. It will stay with you forever." Isn't that the truth?

How badly did I want the details?

Did I want the truth about who he really was, what he had done?

If he had cheated, could I handle seeing his words texted to another woman, or worse, what if there were pictures?

No.

The answer was no. Despite how curious I was, I didn't want to see what was on his computer because I wasn't sure I could recover from what I would find. Besides, I remembered from a former relationship with a narcissistic, compulsive liar that I had wasted months trying to catch him in the act when my gut had known the truth all along. Following that relationship, I had always wished I had the courage to trust my instincts and leave rather than waste time trying to find evidence to *justify* my departure. This time, I would trust my instinct to leave. I went home to begin sorting through our house to determine what was mine versus his, get it packed up, and then do what with it? I still wasn't quite sure. I had nowhere to live and hadn't quite figured out anything beyond buying boxes and packing tape.

Tom had lied to me. I didn't have all the details about the depth of his falsehoods, but I knew they were there. Although I had decided against the spyware, I did discover that several of our good friends and his colleagues were no longer friends with him on social media. I made several phone calls to mutual friends and even to numbers I didn't recognize on his cell phone bill. Mostly, I was stonewalled by those who had worked with him. It seemed obvious to me that they must know something they weren't allowed to discuss. With my prior experience working in HR, I knew that anytime there was an investigation related to an employee, the first thing I would tell any employee I questioned was, "This conversation needs to remain confidential, and failure to do so can result in disciplinary action." These employees were only following instructions in order to maintain their employment status, and I couldn't take it personally.

The hardest call I had to make was to the wife of Tom's former boss, as she was one of my good friends. I was worried she wouldn't take my call since it seemed no one associated with the company could talk to me. However, she answered, and I immediately started with, "I know you can't tell me anything about Tom, but I wanted to call you to let you know that I found out he was terminated for something and lied to me about it. I don't know what's going on, but I'm working on finding out. I hope you and I can still be friends despite your husband working for the company, and if you are open to it, I promise not to ask either of you questions about Tom or about anything that happened." She sounded relieved on the other end when she agreed that our friendship could continue. It sounded like she may have been crying when she apologized for not being able to speak on behalf of anything that happened related to Tom, but she was open to maintaining a friendship with me. She also sounded relieved to know that I was leaving Tom while he was out of town.

With this friendship out of jeopardy, I doubled down and looked further outside the immediate circle to see if anyone had the information I was itching for. I was desperate to give myself an explanation for *why* my gut was telling me I had to leave. There was no time to wait for information to ensure I was making the right decision or to cry, feel sorry for myself, and freak out—or maybe there was but I just work well under pressure. Perhaps my partial German ancestry runs so thick that when I have a job to do, I can focus on nothing other than the process and efficiency required to get it done. Setting emotions aside and getting shit done might be in my DNA.

Karina, one of my dearest friends since high school, cleared her schedule for the week so she could come over and assist. We've known each other since 7th grade, but we became great friends during high school and then were roommates in college. Between then and our forties, where we were at this stage, we certainly had experienced some bumps and bruises. Family and work take time away from an adult friendship, but mostly it was me being an asshole that had caused the most damage. We eventually worked through it and came out still with a strong bond on the other side. Karina is one of those people who could forgive almost anything. She always thought about other people, and, oh my god, could she make me laugh. Laughing around Karina was a guarantee…even when I was in the middle of what we had dubbed a "midnight move," losing my long-term relationship, my home (that I *just* finished remodeling), and questioning my own sanity.

Dare I say, she almost made the process fun. We got out an old whiteboard and propped it up on my oversized kitchen island. Taking breaks from packing, we would sit on the stuffed zebra-striped bar stools I had found in a haughty resale store in Scottsdale and wrote down any ideas we had about what Tom could have done on a stack of Post-it Notes. The board conjured up detective movie vibes where they would tack pictures on a bulletin board in the briefing room and tie strings from the victim to the suspects as the mystery grew closer to being solved. Slowly, I received bits and pieces of information from various sources, and we would move the Post-its between columns we created on the whiteboard for true, untrue, or unknown. We jotted down ideas like 'murder' or 'embezzlement' but quickly surmised if these specific hypotheses were true, Tom would have been arrested (we hoped). Since he hadn't been arrested, only fired, we dialed down our imaginations a tad. It was funny the places the mind will go when you have a vast landscape of unknowns to work with. All that human resources background only fueled my creativity since I had seen in real life the assortment of weird shit people get fired for.

    Thanking a god I didn't believe in that I had someone with me during this process. Honestly, Karina could be described as nothing less than an absolute godsend. Here she was calling and scheduling moving companies. Sorting through every pot, pan, and dish in the kitchen. Talking me off a ledge when I wanted to keep the formal dining table I had spent countless hours finding. She asked me, "Do you think he would be mad if he comes home and this table is gone?" I told her, "Of course not; he doesn't care about dining room tables. He didn't have an opinion about anything I did with the house. Plus, he never gets mad at anything." But Karina grounded me by saying, "Is this table worth finding out whether or not he would be mad? We don't know if he is a violent person. We don't know what type of person he is at all. He has done something bad enough to lose his friends and his relationship with you."

She was right. Everything I thought I knew with certainty was now gone. Tom was as much a mystery to me as if I hadn't ever lived with him at all. While I so loved that dining table, I had searched for months to find precisely the right one and then even longer accumulating the most perfect mismatched dining chairs; it wasn't worth a potential confrontation with this man, this stranger. On reflection, it seems a table should have immediately been determined as unimportant. But somehow, it was representative of the amount of effort I had dedicated to this family, at least the family I had thought we were building. Not only did I pour my heart into the physical remodeling of this home, but I had also tried to provide the parenting and discipline that his children lacked so that they could grow into productive members of society. Why I placed all this symbolism into a dining room table we rarely used, I couldn't explain. I decided at that moment if there were any questions about ownership of any material item, I would leave it behind. Possessions were something I didn't need; I needed my family to be safe and to start my healing process. *Life is not about things.*

How did I pull off a move during Tom's week-long fishing vacation? Well, without Karina's help, I'm not sure I could have. But what made it even better is that I normally didn't talk to Tom while he was on his fishing vacations anyway. He was often out of cell service since he didn't have an international calling plan on his phone, and I enjoyed being alone during this week, so I didn't check in during these trips. Introversion for the win! It absolutely worked in my favor once we were furiously boxing and stacking all my belongings. Karina had arranged for the movers to come on Friday, and Tom would be back home on Saturday. My storage unit was rented and ready to receive the boxes and furniture that I would be keeping. Before we started the packing process, I had to disable the interior and exterior security cameras installed around the house.

Even though Tom and I wouldn't talk while he was gone, he was into computers and was always tinkering with new ways to automate the house, and he was always checking the cameras via an app on his phone. I never understood why a house needed to be automated, but perhaps it had something to do with whatever deception he had been pulling off behind my back. He had most of the first floor of the house and the main exterior points of entry and exit covered. I remembered that he had trouble keeping the cameras connected to the internet, so he had to purchase a Wi-Fi extender solely to handle the cameras because they wouldn't stay connected to our regular modem (Or was it a router? Honestly, I don't know the difference!). He had bitched about what a pain in the ass it was to reprogram all the cameras to the extender, and for once, I was grateful I listened to his computer babble. Without disabling the internet to the entire house, I was able to disconnect the extender and, thereby, the cameras, which allowed us to move freely about the house without being watched. We stacked the finished boxes in the garage, outside of view of the cameras, just in case. He was busy fishing in Canada, though; there was no way he was going to take the time to worry about the cameras being down.

By Wednesday night, most of the boxes had been packed, and furniture had been wrapped in plastic and labeled with a colored Post-it Note if it was to be moved. Karina had gone home to spend some time with her family, and I was planning to shower and get a good night's sleep—one of the last I would have in this house. I had one day left before the movers arrived, and I needed a break. There had been no real downtime for me to process my feelings or even figure out some basic logistics on where I was going to stay once the movers finished on Friday. My brain had been worrying non-stop, thinking while my body was busy packing...and I was fried.

To make the timing more complicated, I had accepted that new job and was starting work on Monday. Not merely a new *job*, but I was going to be responsible for spinning up a new *company*. I'd never started a company before, so I was probably getting in over my head, but I had felt daring at the time because everything in my life was so stable. I had needed a challenge.... talk about being careful what you wish for! My whole existence had suddenly become a challenge. While I couldn't think of a worse time for this to happen, I had a pervasive feeling that everything was working out exactly the way it was supposed to. Monday would be like a reset button on my entire life. One short week ago, I thought I was accepting a cool project to give my life depth. A week later, I was at the bottom of the depths and craved 24 hours of downtime to think about where to stay temporarily while finding a long-term home.

It was getting late, and I decided to head to bed for some much-needed sleep, leaving the details to sort out for tomorrow. Once I pulled the covers up and exhaled into a comfortable position on my mattress, I heard an unfamiliar noise coming from downstairs. It was a noise that is hard to describe, kind of like a toy remote control car. Clicking and whirring, then clicking and whirring again. Had all been normal in my life, I probably wouldn't have paid attention and instead gone to sleep. But because my nervous system was on overload, I stood up and pulled my robe nice and tight around my body like it was some type of comfy shield. Thinking more clearly, I took my 9-millimeter out of the nightstand, stuck it in the pocket of my comfy robe, and went downstairs to check it out.

As I made my way down the stairs, it sounded like the noise was coming from the front of the house, near the front door. I paused to listen to the whirrrrr, click, whirrrr, click, thinking I might recognize the sound and laugh at myself for my paranoia, certain I was simply overly tired and on edge. Since I couldn't tell if the noise was coming from inside or outside, I crept towards the window next to the door to peek outside, my gun now in hand and finger next to the trigger. The front den that Tom used as his office was to the left of the stairs and next to the front door. When I approached the front door, it became clear the sound was actually coming from the den. The lights were all out downstairs, but I could see the power light on the security camera in the den, as the camera turned in circles, assessing the room.

Whirrrrr, came from the camera each time it swiveled around on its base. Click was the sound of the infrared responding to the various changes of light between the two doorways into the den. Since I had disabled the Wi-Fi extender to the cameras, I knew they shouldn't be on at all, much less turning on their base surveying the room. The only possible way that could happen was if Tom had logged into the cameras, noticed they were not an active feed, and programmed them to the other Wi-Fi router remotely from his phone. It would have taken a considerable amount of time, which I had inaccurately bet he wouldn't spend from his cabin on the lake. From his phone, he could control the cameras and was rotating this one remotely to view all areas of the room. It sent shivers down my spine, to think he could probably see me standing there in my comfy robe, gun in hand, processing what was going on. Even though I knew he was thousands of miles away at that moment, I felt him watching me, and it was like he was present in the room. Initially, I felt paralyzed, like prey. It felt like I had been standing there for hours, but I finally regained my bearings and ran upstairs to the master bedroom. It felt silly to be running away from an inanimate object, but I couldn't stop shaking as I locked myself inside the bedroom upstairs.

Immediately, I whipped out my cell and called Karina to tell her what had happened and how creeped out I was. I thought that telling the story would make me realize I was overreacting so I could calm down and go to sleep. Karina was much more rational about the situation, and before I could even finish the story without skipping a beat, she said, "Pack a bag quickly and get the hell out of there, *now*! Come to my house; you can sleep on the couch."

I tried to argue, rationalizing that he wasn't even in the same state as me. Sure, it was creepy that he was looking around the house via the cameras, but what could he possibly do about it? Karina reminded me of how little we actually understood about this man. Maybe he would send someone over to the house or fly home early and catch me while I was still in the house. I quickly realized she was right, and this wasn't the time to try to prove anything. My heart had been pounding non-stop since I saw the camera whirling around, and I knew it was time to go. There was no time to be sad or think about the fact that there would be no more nights sleeping in my bed, in the house I had worked so hard trying to make perfect. That is the funny thing about perfection…it doesn't exist. It was almost comical that I had spent months creating my idea of a perfect home while all the time I was living with someone I didn't even know. But I didn't have time to ponder that. I threw my necessities into an overnight bag and jumped in my SUV, grateful Karina was a night owl and had taken my call.

Even though it was a Wednesday night, everyone at Karina's house was still awake. Her husband was on the phone when I arrived, telling someone all about the incident with the cameras at my house. He was all frenzied, explaining that Tom was an ex-military sniper, and now he was going to fly home and find me at their house, and his family would be in danger. As he told this exaggerated story, I raised my eyebrows at Karina. "Tom is a former sniper now?" I asked. She said that Tom had told her husband he had been a sniper when he was in the military. I confirmed that he had been in the military but had not been a sniper. We added that to the list of lies and incongruences we had been tallying up over the past few days. It finally occurred to me that there was a camera in the kitchen where Karina and I had set up the whiteboard covered in Post-its. We had stood at the kitchen island multiple times, throwing out guesses and theorizing about each one. Had Tom been watching and listening via that camera the whole time? That thought led to another round of shivers and an immense sense of relief that I was not physically in that house any longer. Karina's husband finally calmed down (and let me stay), and I settled in on the family room couch to attempt to get some sleep.

Sleep didn't come easy that night or the next. Fear was starting to creep in as the date came closer for Tom to come home. The camera incident was benign, but it remained as a reminder that I shouldn't let my guard down and couldn't allow myself to feel safe yet. I had never seen him angry or get physically aggressive toward anyone, so a part of me didn't feel this fear was logical. But I felt it every day anyway, like a lingering presence. I started carrying my gun with me everywhere I went, thankful to live in Arizona, where it was fully legal to do so. It was like my blankie, providing some level of comfort as long as I didn't think rationally about Tom's military training for too long. While his sniper story may have been fabricated, I had been to the shooting range with him often enough to know he would outsmart and outperform me with a gun any day of the week.

The point of moving while Tom was on vacation was primarily to avoid giving him the opportunity to lie more, but it was also done strategically so that he wouldn't have the chance to ask me how I found out about his double life. In the days following that fated happy hour, I called anyone and everyone who might be able to tell me what happened. Mostly, I received more of the same vague refusals to share information that had originally tipped me off. Between little pieces of information given up (mostly on accident) and some digging through Tom's things in the last days at home before the creepy camera ran me out, I had figured out enough about his escapades with other women. My priority was protecting my sources of the little bit of information I had, and I wasn't a skilled deceiver like he was. Even though I expected him to do nothing but lie to me if I ever spoke with him again, I still knew that I wouldn't be able to blatantly lie to him if he started throwing out names of individuals who may have revealed his coveted secret. So, there was some relief when Tom never contacted me. Though I knew he had seen the house through the cameras, there was no inquiry about paintings missing from the walls, why I wasn't at home, or any of the things he would have been able to piece together from the security cameras.

On Friday, I went back to the house to meet the movers. I hadn't been back since the camera incident and had no intention of returning after that day. My suitcases were packed, and the movers had taken all my furniture to a storage unit I had rented. You would think I would run out of the house and away from the creepy cameras and all the lies. Instead, I went through the house one final time and bid farewell to some of the pieces that I would have loved to take with me. After the movers left, I ran the vacuum because my OCD wouldn't allow me to leave the indents in the carpet from the furniture that was now removed.

My stomach was in knots thinking that Tom might try to contact me after he returned to this now half-empty home. The best solution I could come up with to eliminate that possibility was to leave a note asking him not to contact me. I outlined that I had paid all the next month's bills from the joint account and would close it out and send him his money once the checks had cleared. I decided not to address what he had done, other than saying, "I know what you did. I have no interest in talking to you; don't contact me." Once the note was placed in the middle of the kitchen island, I knew it was time to go. There was nothing else for me here. The house felt cold as I locked up for the last time.

Surprisingly, Tom returned from his trip on Saturday, and I didn't hear a peep. There was no apology, no acknowledgment of what he had done...nothing. Don't get me wrong, I was happy he didn't contact me; it was what I had asked for. On the other hand, I also felt I deserved an apology. Jesusfuckingchrist, doesn't the average human being usually offer some form of apology, especially after five years together? Apparently, a sociopath doesn't feel sorry for blowing up your life or have any empathy for that matter, so I guess it makes sense.

As the weeks and months moved on I realized that my new nickname for Tom, "the Sociopath" was actually accurate. Tom was a textbook *sociopath*. The more I learned, the more stupid I felt. He had cheated not once, not twice, but the entire five years we had been dating. His infidelities hadn't been solely casual encounters but included calculated sexual harassment toward women who worked for him. Eventually, that had gotten him fired. It took some time to dig up information because of the company's gag order on everyone. Having been in HR, I understood that was required to safeguard the company. The beauty of it was Tom had been up to his tricks for so long that there were a lot of people who had past knowledge of his transgressions. Many of those people were no longer employed by the company or bound to their rules. Some were from prior workplaces who had no ties to that company anyway. One by one, the stories had come trickling in from a variety of sources. People heard that I had left Tom and was looking for information, and my texts and Facebook Messenger were dinging with new tidbits.

When I went through Tom's desk while packing, I found his termination paperwork and discovered he pretended to still go to work after losing his job. Every day, leaving the house at the same time, probably to buy time to figure out what lie he was going to tell me about his newly unemployed status. He had lied intricately and with great detail, without regard for anyone in his path. Perhaps he was also a sex addict because I couldn't see any other reason that he would risk his family, a job that he loved, and a very healthy and relied-upon income stream for quick sexual encounters. He preyed upon the weak, young, or needy types who were more likely to comply and less likely to report his unacceptable behavior. Those young girls in his employ, making minimum wage, barely scraping by on the meager salary offered in their line of work. Tom had a solution for that. Suck his dick, and your phone bill might get paid. Eventually, I even heard a rumor that he had bought one of the girls a car. A fucking car! How the hell did he pay for a car for another person, right under my nose, without me knowing? Either she was great in bed or maybe threatened to tell someone, but for some reason, she suddenly showed up to work in a Mercedes, Tom's favorite brand of auto. Another one he had snuck into our house when I was out of town *while the kids were home*. Even though I was long gone, it made me sick. The sheer number of people who had the information I so desperately needed was both relieving and repulsive. I'm glad there were so many people outside the gag order to help me piece it together, but also, I felt like a complete fucking idiot when it appeared I was one of the only humans on the planet who didn't know who this man was. One of his girls even started attending the same CrossFit gym as me, either intentionally or ironically, I'm not sure which.

It wasn't only about sex, though. Tom lied about everything. He cheated people out of money. He was dishonorably discharged from the military (I never figured out what for), but he always talked about his time in service as if he were some kind of war hero. He lied about his financial situation. He lied about his kids and ex-wives. There almost wasn't a topic I could find that he didn't lie about.

One night, when I was out to dinner with friends, someone I didn't even recognize approached me. They knew I had dated Tom, and we had broken up, so they felt they could share their secrets with me now. They pulled up a chair to our table in the middle of the restaurant to enlighten us even more. Luckily, I was with friends who knew Tom and weren't tired of the topic, so I excused myself and went to the bathroom. As much as I had been desperate for information in those first few days, I couldn't escape the information now. It was starting to feel like I was a hostage to my past in this city, with negativity lurking in the shadows and popping out unpredictably just to throw me off my game.

I had lived in the same house as a sociopath, introduced him to my family, had my daughter under the same roof as this predator, and had unsuspectingly planned my future with this man. Either I was extremely fucking ignorant, or he was far smarter than I gave him credit for to pull off the tangled web of an entirely fake life. It gave me chills to think I had trusted him...this man I really didn't know at all.

♥

New Job, Who Dis?

During the midnight move, my clothes were one of the few things not sent off to storage. They were neatly stacked in the back of my SUV, still on their hangers, fresh from my custom-built closet. Man, I loved that closet. Everything organized by color, tucked and tidy, precisely the way I liked it—basically the exact opposite of stacked in the back of an SUV. Over the next several nights, I bounced between various friend's and family's homes. A couch here, a spare room there. I was now living in areas smaller than the aforementioned closet. Never in a million years would I have pictured my life taking this turn. The offers for a temporary place to stay rolled in. Messages from friends with extra space for me to crash kept me feeling grateful during such a weird time of transition.

The Monday after my move-out, I started my new business opportunity. Under different circumstances, I would have been stressed about that new undertaking. It would be my responsibility to create the firm from the ground up. We didn't even have a name for the company yet, so there was quite a task looming in front of me, and I was more than ready to throw myself into the mountain of work required. But I wasn't nervous, stressed, or feeling much of anything.

Maybe numb...I was, at best, numb as I parked my car at the new office I would be driving to every day.

Driving 'from where?' was a question I couldn't answer yet. As I looked back to my parking space, I could see the pile of clothes on hangers in the back of the SUV. Suddenly, my heart started racing because the damn windows weren't tinted dark enough. It looked like a homeless person was living in my car. Oh, wait. I guess that would be technically correct; I was homeless. The rear of my car directly faced the windows of the office building, and I pictured everyone inside peering out and seeing right through my facade. I felt hauntingly naked and quickly peered down to ensure I was, in fact, wearing clothing.

Here, I was expected to present viable ideas on building an agency, how to market and grow in a competitive and over-saturated industry, and how to support their other existing business lines. These people were supposed to trust me to set up a business for them, and *I didn't even know where I was going to live*. There was no way I would leave my car here in one of the front spots, closest to the building, crammed to the gills with the evidence of my new gypsy existence.

After a deep breath, I retraced my steps back to the vehicle. Then I parked it further away in the parking lot, silently telling myself that no one was looking out the windows and I had an overactive imagination. Deep down, I knew I wasn't really a loser, but I felt like others would think so if they knew the current state of my personal affairs. Literally, 100% of my success was going to hinge on assessing other people; who would be a good client and which candidate would most successfully meet the needs of our clients, yet I couldn't assess a man I saw every fucking day. What wrong turn did I take that this was my reality?

This cynicism tempered any excitement I felt over the next few months as we created and massaged this idea for our firm. I normally would have loved being a part of this process, and I did love it, but in a way that was like being happy for a close friend. It wasn't *my* story; it was an out-of-body experience that I was only partially present for. Not in a crackhead kind of way; I wasn't all zoned out and drooling during meetings or anything. But it was like having the radio on in the background, and the station you have tuned in was a repetitive mantra of;

You suck. Don't trust yourself. What the fuck do you know? You're an idiot. Why would anyone trust your decisions, you don't know anything. You've been duped before, and it will happen again, dummy.

Every move I made, I ran it through this filter, which caused me to not speak my truth, not trust my judgment, and not celebrate my wins. With each step I took, I was waiting for the other shoe to drop, for the rug to be pulled out from under me. Instead of running forward and embracing this opportunity, I was teetering like a toddler learning how to walk for the first time. One step....stop wait. Assess the situation. Has anyone pushed me or pulled my floor from under me? No. Okay, one more step....stop wait.

To make it worse, my personality was divided into two camps, like Thing 1 and Thing 2 in the Dr. Suess story. Thing One says, "Suck it up, buttercup, you got off easy. It's not like anything very terrible happened. No one died (that you know of). Nothing happened to your daughter. So what? You wasted five years of your life. You're only 41, get on with it." But Thing Two says, "Trust no one. Men are predators and will always hurt you. You should know this by now. No one is that nice in real life, and you should have known he was a fake. That's what you get for being stupid."

Ugh. Why were these thoughts constantly prevalent, haunting my every waking hour? Why couldn't I move past this?

Perhaps because I lost my identity. Not like my wallet was stolen, and someone was running around with my credit card. I mean it in the sense of my reasons for being *who I am*. When this clusterfuck with Tom happened, my only daughter was preparing for her final year of college. She was born while I was still in college, so my entire adult life had been centered around being a mom. So, on that Saturday in June, when she was moving into her own apartment, it was the first time I'd ever lived in a home without my child.

Then, that following Tuesday, I accepted the job offer to help start this new company. With almost no agency experience or technical recruiting experience. So, I was walking away from (or losing my identity) as being an expert in my field. Fast forward to Thursday of the same damned week. That was the fateful Thursday I found out that Tom had been fucking around the entire five years we had been dating. Sure gives a new meaning to 'Thirsty Thursday.'

So, in the course of one week, I literally started my life over. At 41, I felt I was no longer a mom. I was single again and had moved out of my freshly remodeled house that I had planned to live in for years to come. And I was starting a new career.

In some ways, I feel like there was no other option than to pull up my big girl panties and keep moving. At first, I was merely taking action to stay afloat. Packing my things had a deadline, and starting this job had a deadline. Once the adrenaline settled down, there was an emptiness that I wasn't prepared for. When I didn't feel empty, I would bounce between sadness, anger, and, oddly, fear. I'd never feared Tom before, but now I carried my 9-millimeter religiously. The idea of running into him unnerved me to the bone.

Sometimes, out of the blue, I would find myself crying for no reason. I'd never been a crier or a feeler. Feelings are like crayons to a coloring book and I had been living in black and white for a long time. It was hard to navigate what I was feeling because while I was hurt, there was a part of me that was relieved. My sadness was saying goodbye to an idea and knowing I would never see it come to fruition, but it wasn't the deep heartache that comes with losing your true love. Deep down, I knew I had been settling, not wholeheartedly pursuing all that I knew I wanted and deserved. Instead, I found someone nice (or so I thought) and built a life, making excuses for why I couldn't have the rest of it.

Nice is more important than looks, money, a great sex life, etc.

I can't have it all. I need to sacrifice something in order to date a nice guy.

With all these conflicting emotions, it was easier to go numb. Numbness wasn't an intentional plan that I came to, like, "Hey self - do we want to deal with all this shit, process it, sit with it, and actually heal? Or do we want to stuff it down until we don't think about it anymore and kick that can down the road?" I think my subconscious did what it felt needed to be done, and 'checking out' was kind of my default mode.

The unpredictability of what I was going to feel and when made me suit up in my armor each day so that I could get through my to-do items. The thing about going numb is that sometimes you fool yourself into thinking you have healed when, really, you stuffed it all so far down you think it's gone. But it's still there, lurking, waiting for the moment you are least expecting, and then, bam. Some random horrible thought enters your head, or your self-esteem suddenly disappears into thin air for no reason, and it's coming from that pain monster you stuffed down in the cracks.

While my brain constantly told me how inferior I was, my exterior composure remained cool. For several weeks, I was pet-sitting for various friends while I looked for someplace to live. The house that Tom bought was in the neighborhood that I had lived in for years. It was *my* neighborhood, not his, and I felt slices of anger that I could no longer live in that part of town. My gun-toting paranoia would be constantly activated if I had to concern myself with running into him while getting gas, groceries or during any number of errands.

Renting was a challenge after my home remodeling project. I went from picking out tumbled travertine flooring to viewing rentals with smudged paint, sticky appliances, and worn carpet. Since I was a child, I've always been compulsively neat. There's a certain soothing feeling that cleaning and organizing brings to my soul. Realistically, having things in order provided me with a sense of control I couldn't otherwise satisfy. Finally, I walked into one house listed by the owner in nearly pristine condition. Even though a few of the listings in my old neighborhood were larger, I chose this smaller home in a different suburb of the valley, where I'd be unlikely to run into Tom. I signed the lease and started to feel a little less loser-y, knowing that I was no longer homeless. Maybe, just maybe, things were making a turn for the better.

Looking back, it seems strange that I had been so determined to move out immediately before having the facts of Tom's infractions. Something I couldn't see at the time because I was living inside so many walls was that I existed in fight or flight mode. There seemed to be an innate expectation that men would do bad things that would prevent me from ever trusting or relying on one. When I was younger, that manifested itself into a bitchy exterior. In college, I was the one always ready for a fight. Men always flocked to Karina because of her model-esque appearance, but I was always in-between, growling and barking like a little chihuahua guard dog. I drove around in a truck (because I thought that made me tougher) with a bumper sticker that read, "I wasn't born a bitch, men like you make me that way." Eventually, I grew out of that yappy chihuahua phase, but I never opened my heart and mind to trust anyone with a Y chromosome. It was like I was always sleeping with my running shoes on, ready to make my escape the minute they would fuck up. And they would because they were men.

♥

Rock Bottom

After a several months of working for the investors, we had an operational technical recruitment firm. Sure, the business was functioning, but we were struggling to bring consistent revenue in the door. As much as I tried to keep my personal issues out of my work life, it is hard to have your confidence completely shaken without some impact on your professional life. The persona that I'd created for myself over the years was a bit rough around the edges - the type who should be tough and bounce back quickly from any transgressions because she doesn't give a fuck about anyone else. But that was the razor wire I wound myself with to protect the fact that I'm actually a highly sensitive person.

Having my trust violated so deeply the year before set me on a healing journey that I previously didn't realize I needed. But first, I had to hit rock bottom. For a good year after my midnight move, I turned to work and alcohol (not usually at the same time) to distract me from the deep self-analysis and improvements I needed to make. In the mornings, I'd pull myself out of bed with the promise of a sugary latte to break my comatose state. Forget morning runs or the gym...the muscle I'd built up in CrossFit atrophied at an alarming rate. The extra pounds appeared as my legs started resembling tree trunks topped with an ass made of cottage cheese. Usually at work no later than 7 am, I'd drown myself in anything and everything that didn't have to do with my personal life. I never left work early, but no matter how long I lingered, it would be inevitable that I would need to return home in the evening alone.

Throughout my life, I'd had short stints of singleness, but the longest amount of time I'd spent not in a relationship was maybe six months. It had already been longer than that since I had moved out while the sociopath was on his fishing vacation. Rather than use this time constructively, you know, maybe sit with my thoughts and work on forgiving and healing...I began a routine of opening a bottle of wine and my laptop to continue working while Netflix-binging on shows I never previously had time to watch. *Gilmore Girls* and *Dexter* accompanied me late into the evenings until I drank enough wine to fall asleep. My brain would sometimes suggest that I deal with my issues, and I'd wonder why I was so closed off to love. While I had been in relationships continuously, I hadn't opened my heart to anyone.

As long as I could remember, I had built up walls around me, always expecting the worst from men. Part of it was merely my personality, I thought. Most of my friends had gotten married in our early twenties, after having dreamt about what their dresses would look like, how many kids they wanted, blah blah blah. That had never appealed to me growing up. Maybe that was built into my destiny, or a product of some of the experiences endured before I hit maturity. Regardless, these weren't dreams that I'd had; they were only expectations from society that I thought were my obligation to fulfill. Honestly, in hindsight I should have never gotten married. Sure, I would have dated my ex-husband, and had a long-term relationship, but there was no reason I should have sealed that deal with a government contract. Why did I ever allow societal norms to dictate my life? I should have explored this deeper, but I don't think my heart was ready for it.

While I am supposed to be hitting rock bottom here, and believe me, I was, but OMG, why had I never watched *Gilmore Girls* before? Sage had jokingly told me it was loosely based on our life...and she was spot on. I've never felt more kinship with a fictional character than with Lorelai Gilmore! This show was like the only light in a very dark year and a way for me to feel like my daughter was still in the house, even though she had never even lived in the new rental I was in.

Weekends were more of the same, but at least I intermittently made plans with friends to break up the monotony. But there were plenty of other weekends when I only left my house to go to Starbucks in the morning. If I allowed myself to analyze my situation, there was a niggling feeling that I'd have to come to terms with my past and learn to forgive. Not related to Tom per se, but I'd have to go so much further back to truly understand why I'd ever allowed myself to attract a sociopath in the first place.

It was a sad mix of depression, stress, and a lack of motivation to give a shit about myself. There was more than enough time for me to go to the gym or a hike, meal prep for the upcoming week, or go to therapy - but I couldn't bring myself to do anything worthwhile. It felt like I was swimming in a current; I was working hard to stay in the same place.

♥

Winds of Change
The turning point came unsuspectingly one day when I was scrolling LinkedIn, cyberstalking candidates I

thought might be a good fit for a position one of our clients had hired us to fill, and I came across an article about a company called Remote Year. At the time, this company was a relatively new concept. They put together year-long, multi-continent travel agendas, mostly for gap year students who wanted to travel the world before sacrificing themselves to the corporate gods for a lifetime of dull suit-wearing and chasing of unattainable corporate metrics. The travel company was an interesting concept, and as I clicked on some related articles, I realized that this wasn't exclusively for gap year students. There were plenty of companies catering to digital nomads, aka people who don't 'live' anywhere; they work from a laptop wherever they are and travel around wherever they want to be in the moment. It piqued my curiosity, but I quickly dismissed it when I thought about all the 'in person' events I had scheduled, cold calling that required me to visit local businesses, and managing the team who were currently required to show up and work in the office. Shrugging it off as a cool concept, I returned to my search for my mystery rockstar candidate. There was no way I could travel the world and run this recruitment agency, so why spend any more time getting sucked down that rabbit hole?

 The thought may have passed through my consciousness a few more times, but I didn't pay attention. We desperately needed to hire someone to head our sales team, in order to get our revenue up. We were missing our anticipated sales by miles, and

I felt responsible since I should have recognized that the revenue targets in our first year were completely unrealistic. As a somewhat socially awkward introvert, sales was an area that I couldn't pull my weight. Give me systems and processes to create, and I'm in my wheelhouse (oops, my German is showing again), but make me go to networking events to mingle and smile, and my best efforts will fall short like the episode of *Big Bang Theory* when Sheldon gets fired for introducing himself as "an actual real scientist" to his new boss.

After some searching, we had two candidates in the final stages for our VP of Sales role. They each had different strengths, which made it a tough choice because we needed a mix of both backgrounds, but I had to make a recommendation on which *one* would be chosen. It was Friday, and I needed to make my decision by Monday. I grew increasingly stressed and overwhelmed, and could no longer visualize this venture as being successful. We lacked a real 'why' to our business other than to make money. Profit can never be your only why. Deep down, I knew that I needed to be a stronger leader to create that authentic reason for existing and build the momentum for our team. But every day, I was living with the frequency of anxiety running like an electric current right under the surface. In the morning, I'd start dousing it with caffeine to jump-start the battery and end the day, drowning it in wine to turn it off. I wasn't performing at my highest intellectual or emotional level.

So that Friday found me feeling particularly fried. I struggled through most of the day knowing I needed to pick a candidate for our sales role but couldn't wrangle enough clarity in my thoughts to validate a choice. Probably in an effort to avoid making a decision, I started scrolling the internet for available hotel rooms on the beach in California - a six-hour drive away. I felt an overwhelming urge to hear the waves crash and do nothing more than sit on the beach. One more weekend spent alone with a bottle of wine and the *Gilmore Girls* and I was certain to lose my mind (no offense Lorelai). It was only March, so the beach would still be cold, but I didn't care. My life hadn't really been a life for a while, and each day had become a predictable pattern of self-abuse. Frustration lingered at the end of each day, long after I'd left my office feeling guilty for not single-handedly turning our firm into an overnight sensation. Doubt no longer crept into my mind to harass me with those negative questions about being good enough; it lived there full time. Of course, I put on appearances and acted like all was well and I was moving on, but something wasn't right or healthy about me. I knew it without knowing it.

Not one to typically leave early or even take my earned vacation time, everyone was shocked when I walked out of work that Friday early. It wasn't even 4 o'clock when I closed my computer and left the building. On my way out, one of my colleagues stopped me and asked if I was okay. When I nodded and said

I was driving to California for the weekend, alone, he squinted his eyes and hesitated. It was obviously out of character for me, but he let it be, probably not wanting to probe any further on the off chance I'd sit down and start pouring out my life story.

With the SUV packed up, I put on my favorite playlist and headed west a few hours before sundown. There is nothing more freeing than the open road, in a car alone, so you can turn the music up to the volume of your choosing and scream-sing along with your favorite road trip tunes. For me, that means music turned up as loud as it can go without blowing the speakers. I was blessed with a voice intended for a monotone mathematics professor, so the music needs to drown out the sound of my jubilantly loud and equally terrible singing.

I arrived at the beach in record time, but I wasn't feeling up for going out alone on a Friday night, so I retreated to my hotel room for an early sleep. While I had traveled alone plenty of times for work trips, I had never once traveled alone for pleasure. It felt weird not to have any particular plans and no one to check in with. Most of all, it felt strange to walk around with no one to talk to. Doing everything by myself was the norm at home, but on the beach in California, I realized that I was uncomfortable with myself in that space. What was up with that? The weekend was mostly an unmemorable blur of walking the beach, ducking into surf shops if I saw something interesting, and trying to avoid the crowds of

Trump protestors crawling the bursting intersections of the Pacific Coast Highway. Punctuating the mundane were the hours I could sit on the relatively empty beach and just be. It was barely warm enough to walk around and the wind blowing off the water non-stop made the beach downright chilly. Bundled for warmth, but with shoes off and toes in the sand, I stared into the surf, waiting for answers. To what questions, I wasn't even entirely sure, but I knew the answers were there in the water. I imagined throwing all of my burdens into the ocean and letting the frothy waves consume them.

Had you been a private detective following my every move, you would have never guessed I changed my life that weekend. It was most certainly not visible to an outside observer, but on the inside, something had changed. This was the first weekend I had actually *spent* with myself.

Not drinking.
Not binging on Netflix.
Not out with friends.
Not burying myself in work.

Sitting alone with myself and truly looking inside made me realize I didn't like what I saw. In a moment of clarity, I knew what needed to be done. There would be no more excuses, no more waiting, and no more denying that I needed to heal.

Downsizing

Normally, my rush to get to the office in the morning was stress-induced. I'd wake up around 2 am, sweating about job orders we couldn't seem to find the right candidates for or the unrealistic revenue projections that were set for our first year in business. My heart rate would spike while I would think to myself:

Why the fuck did you think you could come anywhere near this number in revenue before you even had a single client? You don't know what the fuck you are doing! Someone with more experience would have known better. You better get your ass in gear and figure it out.

That would lead to a few hours of tossing and turning before finally giving up and dragging myself to the shower. There was a time, years ago, when I would pop out of bed before the crack of dawn to go for a run before my day started. No longer. My heavy eyelids and increasingly heavier backside would reluctantly slip through the morning routine of shower, makeup, clothing and then autopilot to the nearest Starbucks. By the time I hit the office door, my step had quickened more out of anxiety than anything else. Convinced that some dire consequence would befall me if I weren't in my office before 7 am, I had given up any healthy or balanced morning routine.

That Monday morning was different. When I returned to work after the trip to California, there was a purpose in my step as I walked to my boss's office to discuss my recommendations for the sales hire we needed to make. No longer avoiding the decision, I was actually excited to share my newly percolated idea. My eyelids were not heavy, in fact, had I been able to see myself, I probably had the bright sparkle of excitement in my eyes.

"I think we should hire them both," I eagerly started off with. "We don't have the budget for them both, so let's give one of them the VP of Sales salary, and let's hire the other one for my role and give them *my* salary." As soon as my words hit the air, I saw his jaw open and hang in silence for a moment. "Wait...where are *you* going?" he asked. With full confidence, though not really knowing if he would agree to my plan, I replied, "We have an open recruiter role, so I can take a pay cut to fill that position...*if* you will let me work remotely while I travel around the world for the next year."

After he processed this information and the fact that the girl who drove the same route to work at the same time each day, stopping at the same Starbucks for the exact same drink, had actually asked him to travel the world, he agreed. "I think this will be a life-changing personal growth experience for you," he said. We would hire both candidates and demote me. It was probably a no-brainer for him, other than being somewhat old school in thinking that people needed to be physically present in the workplace. Agreeing to let me work remotely was a huge win and I was grateful he was willing to take the risk on me. But in return, he was getting two solid leadership candidates, and we were filling the recruiting role with talent we were struggling to find.

In a few short months, I would join a travel group of working professionals traveling together in Europe, like the one I had read about on LinkedIn and dismissed as an impossibility for me. (Doesn't the universe work in mysterious ways, setting an idea in motion even when you aren't quite ready to take action?) Each month, our group would move locations, and the travel company had already vetted things like coworking spaces, Wi-Fi speeds, and safety. They would make all my reservations for me, so all I had to do was show up and get on my flight. Around the holidays, I would return to Phoenix and work in the office until I left for the next leg of the trip in January. Everything seemed to be coming together perfectly.

Almost everything. If only getting my daughter on board with this idea was as easy. "Are you having a mid-life crisis?" Sage asked incredulously. She could not understand why in the world I would want to leave the good ol' U.S. of A. Logic has always appealed to her, so I tried explaining my rationale on the timing, "You're graduating from college and getting ready for your adult life. In another year or so, you will probably be getting married or popping babies out. If that happens, I won't want to leave the country for an extended period, so I need to go *now*." She didn't understand why I needed to leave the country at *any* point in time.

She didn't get the wanderlust gene and wasn't even slightly interested in my bribe to bring her to Prague. "Your 21st birthday is coming up in August. I can fly home for it, or even better, fly you out to me for a week. I'll be in Prague, and it would be an amazing way to spend your birthday." Surely, any 21-year-old would jump at the chance to spend a week in Prague for their birthday. Not my daughter. "Ew. Why would I want to spend hours flying across the ocean? I hate flying over water." I guess that is a hard no. How could someone not want to go to Prague? I mean, that specific city wasn't on my bucket list, but if someone offered me a free trip, I would absolutely take it.

There had always been a curiosity inside me to visit other countries and learn more about how people communicated and lived. Spanish had fascinated me when I was younger, and I had taken classes starting from 7th grade all the way into college. Even after all those years, I still wasn't fluent. My dream had been to participate in a foreign exchange program to immerse myself in the culture and language. However, taking action on that dream required two things I didn't have: confidence and money. So, in high school, I told myself I'd do it in college, and then in college, I told myself, "Next year, I'll look into it," knowing full well that I was lying through my teeth. Then I found out I was pregnant with Sage, and the thought of travel was pushed from my mind. I was only concerned with finishing school and working as many jobs as I needed to so that I could raise my daughter. For many years, I lived at the bottom of Maslow's pyramid for the hierarchy of needs; survival. Go to work, pay bills, repeat. How many fucking years of my life was I caught in this cycle? The thought occurred to me now that I may have set the wrong example for Sage. Did I, in actuality, want her to work all the time and not enjoy life? How would she know it was okay to do things that set your soul on fire if she watched me sell my soul for a paycheck for all those years?

Sage knew I hadn't ever acted on my desire to travel when I was younger, but she couldn't understand why I *still* felt like I needed to go. Which was fair. My predictable routine life certainly hadn't raised her to have wanderlust in her heart or head. This need to go somewhere new, to wake up in a new location or to get off a plane and feel exhilarated by the foreign dialect humming all around you. Suddenly, I longed for these experiences as I felt imprisoned by my dull, routine life. It was getting more difficult to pull myself out of bed each day, knowing that this day would look exactly like the 62 before it. Maybe a new destination would provide some meaning or purpose, so I wouldn't need the extra shot of stimulant that three Starbucks a day provided me. Anticipating this new digital nomad lifestyle was like lifting the blanket of depression physically off my body so I could move forward again. At that moment, I felt if I stayed in my current life, I would absolutely suffocate.

People pleasing was a bad habit I cultivated over the last forty years. Leaving the country felt like I was casting aside this habit, even if only temporarily, and doing something for *myself* for once. Traveling wasn't for anyone else…it was for **me**. For reasons unknown, once the idea was hatched in my brain, there was no stopping me. Of course, I love my daughter and didn't want to be away from her for several months. I was terrified that something would happen and I wouldn't be able to make it home to her in time. More realistically, I knew that she had lived on her own for a while now, and we would adjust to this new distance perfectly fine. She had tons of local family: her dad, her boyfriend's parents, and grandparents on both sides. Change is hard, but I knew it had always served me well in the past if I embraced it. Sage never cared for change and definitely did not like this idea, but eventually, she at least stopped fighting it.

In preparation for living out of one suitcase, I watched the documentary *Minimalism*. The main gist of the film is reducing consumerism and living with less. After I watched it, I was all pumped up to reduce my personal belongings to a more manageable amount. When I had moved out of the 3,500 square feet I shared with the sociopath (oh, I mean…Tom) and moved into the 1,600 square feet home I occupied by myself, it felt like a major downsizing. Honestly, I was resentful at that time, knowing that because of *his* actions, I was the one having to downsize my life. It had seemed so unfair. But, once I had begun the process of packing up my 1,600 square feet, it suddenly felt like so much extra baggage to cling to so much stuff. Why did I need the box full of stickers that Sage had used to make crafts when she was four years old? The guest bedroom had Sage's old bed that she hadn't slept in since high school. My 3rd bedroom was solely for the dogs...literally, they had their own room! It was so cathartic to start cleaning and clearing. The goal in the documentary was to reduce personal clothing articles to 33 items, which seemed like a ridiculously low number. For shits and giggles, I decided to go wild on my closet to see what number of items remained. Until about five years before this endeavor, I had always been naturally skinny, wearing a size 0 or 2. As my age crept up, I started gaining a few pounds here and there and couldn't ever shake the extra weight.

"I am going to lose the weight...I swear" – me, every day for the last five years.

Even after joining CrossFit with a cultish fervor and going religiously every day, I still couldn't get down to my pre-40s size. Yet, there I was at age 42, holding on to plastic totes full of jeans and slacks that no longer fit. Every time I looked at those totes, I was filled with shame...insulting myself for giving up my pre-40s running habit, lifting habit, and healthy eating habits. It was probably 20 pounds out of reach to even zip up a single pair of those pants. Suddenly, I was anxious to have those totes removed from my closet and those mental insults removed from my brain. I imagined it felt as good to dump those totes in the donate pile as it would have been to lose that extra 20 pounds. Anything

I hadn't worn or didn't love got dumped in the pile, which grew to be massive!

Rather than causing depression or stress, this process was hugely rewarding. It was so freeing! After the major clean-out, I felt like I had been accepted into some non-conformist club. That is until I counted the remaining things in my closet…there were still over 200 items. Ugh. Well, it was baby steps in the right direction. But how was I possibly going to survive on **one** suitcase? The first leg of my trip would be four months without coming home. I had to fit everything I needed for four countries with different climates into one zippered box the size of two dresser drawers. I'm sure I hyperventilated about this more than once. In the end, I over-packed my suitcase, trying to think of every possible scenario and climate I was heading into.

I imagined beautiful summer weather, unlike the deadly heat of the Arizona sun, with romantic walks on cobblestone pathways. There would be adventurous activities for sure, so I must pack athletic wear. Also, I was certain to take up running again, even though I hadn't lifted one foot out the door for a run in a couple of years now.

Toiletries and hair dryers.

Laptops and converters for all my U.S. electronics.

Layers of clothing.

Comfy shoes and cute shoes.

Four months' worth of skin products and medication.

Nope.

This was not going to fit in one (albeit giant) suitcase with a 50-pound limit. My research had left out how stressful the packing process would be for this first trip. Without having ever been to a single country I was headed to, I had no insight into what I might want to wear. First-world problems. I had become so accustomed to having choices, too many choices to be honest, due to my over-consumerism. I had been so busy filling my life with stuff, *meaningless* stuff. Finally, I had an opportunity to unburden myself and add depth to my life experience, I thought.
   Sorry Tory Burch, I will miss you!
   No more overspending, I promised myself. This trip was going to be an opportunity for me to break some of the bad habits I had accumulated by living in the materialistic United States for too long. Particularly, I wanted to rid myself of the burden of perfectionism. The need to always have the right outfit or the perfect pair of shoes…none of this added purpose or meaning to my life and kept me bound to the golden handcuffs of earning a higher salary. Ultimately, I felt like so much time had been spent (or wasted) chasing the idea of perfection. While I could honestly say that I had a great life, so too could I say that I had continually **failed** at everything I had done. I had *never once* lived up to my expectations to be perfect. So, I will summarize the days leading up to my departure as the "letting go" phase. I hoped the next phase would be titled "embracing imperfection." So I allowed myself one more purchase – a necklace with the word 'imperfect' inscribed on it.

CHAPTER 2
Adios Bitchachos

My flight was boarding at the international terminal at Sky Harbor Airport, and I was waiting to cry. I thought the tears would come when Sage dropped me off at the airport, but I was already boarding, still with dry eyeballs. It would probably hit at the most inopportune time during the flight, and I'd start weeping over my peanut snack bag. Sage graduated college two weeks ago, and all of my stuff was in storage again. I know, here we go again with my stuff in storage…haven't we seen this movie before? It felt so much different this time given it was by choice, not rushed out by movers in a hasty get-a-way.

My flight from Los Angeles to Manchester (UK) was an overnight flight, which was intentionally booked to make the twelve hours on a plane more bearable. Even though I'd never been able to truly sleep on a plane, I'd also never been stuck on one for *twelve* hours. Surely, I would sleep like a baby overnight and not even notice the sardine-like relationship I had with a few hundred other people.

Wrong.

Not that the flight was unbearable, but the mix of excitement and nervousness kept my brain humming along deep into the night. Combined with the fact that my coach seat was far too upright, and I'd never been able to sleep around strangers. Though I faked sleeping to ensure none of my seat neighbors got too chatty. Talking to strangers on the plane is the worst; it's like your ears are being held hostage. Since I had booked the aisle seat, I was at least able to get up and walk around while everyone around me slept. Even though I wore compression socks while traveling, I was still mildly nervous about blot clots. My platelet count was found to be high several years ago, so I tried to be diligent about things like sitting in one place for too long or taking hormones that could cause dangerous blood clots. So, I pretended to sleep when others were awake and paced the aisle when it was safe to avoid unwanted conversation.

Once we landed in Manchester, I collected my bag and boarded a flight with a different airline for the last leg of my trip to Porto, Portugal. When I packed my bag back at home, I had diligently weighed it with a hand scale to see how much I could carry and still remain under the 50-pound limit to avoid overage charges. As I checked in for my next flight, the clerk told me my baggage was overweight and that I would owe those nasty overage fees I had worked so diligently to avoid. Tired from the flight and certain I was correct, I argued with the poor clerk until she explained my error. I had overlooked one tiny detail: the allowable weight is different in other countries and seems to vary by airline. I would have to check each and every flight to determine how many kilos were allowed. For this leg, only 20 kilos (i.e., 44 pounds) was allowable without paying the additional fee. I was 2 kilos over.

Rookie error.

Once I was settled in Portugal, I'd have to slim down my suitcase even further, which seemed impossible at this stage. How would I remain clothed for four months if I had to ship home two more kilos worth of stuff? Not that I even knew how much two kilos worth would equate to. Knowing I was in the wrong, I sulked off to pay my fees and spent the rest of the time in the airport walking up and down the terminal to keep my blood flowing before the next, much shorter flight.

♥

Portugal

Growing up in Arizona, we didn't have public transportation. I mean, it existed, but the infrastructure wasn't robust enough to truly rely on it. Arizona is wide open desert without much of an urban feel. In Phoenix, buildings are single-story stucco, not the glass high rises you see in so many cities with populations over 1.5 million people. City buses ran downtown and through the major portions of the city, but it could take hours to make it from one end of town to the other. In fact, living in the suburbs sometimes meant that buses didn't even run near your neighborhood. It took ages to get a light rail approved, and then once it was built, it was pretty much worthless as the route was confined to one straight line through downtown. Unless you wanted some entertaining people watching and could tolerate an encounter with public urination or intoxication, or more likely, both. Point being, that a car was a necessity in the Valley of the Sun.

Arriving at the airport in Porto and then taking the train would have been foreign to me, even if everyone around wasn't speaking Portuguese. I breathed it all in—the people on the train, the buildings out the window, the announcement in this language I couldn't understand.

Surprisingly, it felt amazing.

Normally, I'd have been annoyed with so many human bodies crammed into the train car. Several of us from the digital nomad group had met up at the airport, and we all had luggage that we were trying to manage so that it wouldn't roll away each time the train car lurched to a stop. The community manager signaled that the next stop was our stop. He would walk us all to the Airbnb apartments the group had rented for us. They had paired up a couple of digital nomads in each apartment, all of which were in different buildings but within walking distance from each other and the city square. Stepping off the train, I leveraged my giant blue suitcase off and onto the beautiful cobblestone street.

Looking around, I saw all the buildings lining the streets on rolling hills, crossed by a Riverwalk. Old buildings sculpted with intricate detail along the windows and roofline, using materials like stone and brick; it couldn't be further from the plain stucco of Arizona. The day was cool, but I started sweating as I worked my way up to my apartment. The big blue suitcase was 50 pounds, which I immediately regretted. What seemed easy to roll through the glossy floors in the airport were now click-clacking heavily on each intricate stone, sometimes the seemingly tiny wheels getting stuck between stones and requiring a little extra muscle to pull them out. I made a mental note to ship some things home as soon as I figured out what things I actually needed to survive several months away from home.

Finally, we reached the apartment I would call home for the next thirty days. I learned a lesson that would continue throughout Europe...these people were not the overly litigious, inclusivity advocates that Americans are. Meaning the apartments have stairs, and if you can't climb the stairs, you are fucked. There were no ramps, no elevators. Hell, the streets and sidewalks even had sizeable chunks missing with no yellow caution tape, cones, or anything. It's like you actually had to open your eyes and pay attention to what you are doing or something.

I liked it.

Except for lugging my suitcase up the stairs to my apartment. After huffing and puffing up to my floor, I saw the cutest little space I could have asked for. Two tiny bedrooms with flower-lined balconies overlooking what felt like an ancient street below. What I thought was really unique was the glass door in the center of the living room, leading out to an enclosed but outdoor patio that housed the washing machine. Just a washing machine, nobody had dryers, what?! It was clean and modern and so freaking adorable. My assigned roommate wasn't home, but I would meet her soon enough.

Part of the benefit of traveling with the digital nomad group was being paired up with other people who were like-minded in the sense that we were all working remotely and wanted to see more of the world. Some had traveled extensively, and others were just getting started, like me. The digital nomad group created a Slack channel so everyone could connect for sightseeing adventures or share quick tips on cool restaurants they had found. Our first night in town was kicked off with a welcome dinner for a large portion of the group that had arrived. As an introvert, I wasn't particularly excited to spend time with a large group of strangers, but I wanted to learn if anyone else in the group was close to my age. Most women in their forties had family or career obligations that prevented them from picking up and traveling the world, so I had expected to be the only one. And the only forty-something I was. That said, two other women in their late thirties were in my group, and one of them happened to be my roommate. I was in luck! I no longer had to worry about being paired up with some recent college grad on gap year who only cared about partying. Is it weird that this was my main concern while dropping everything and flying halfway across the world?

When I met the other mid-thirties traveler at our group dinner the first night, I knew immediately we would be friends. How or why I felt this, I have no idea. Especially coming from me since I'm prepared to dislike most new people I meet. Sometimes, you get a feeling when you meet people. Her name was Grace, and she was from Texas. Grace had a personality as big as her naturally curly hair and was always clad in a seemingly endless supply of patterned yoga pants. She is, without a doubt, an extrovert who has no trouble commanding an audience. As an introvert with an extreme resting bitch face, I think it's serendipitous that I made a friend with opposite qualities. Diversity is critical to pull us from our comfort zones. Before I took off on this trip, I had joked with friends about traveling with a group and how I would probably hate everyone. To counter the negativity, I set a goal to make at least *one* friend during my travels. After dinner, I walked back to my apartment feeling confident that I had met my goal!

Portugal was quite the adjustment for a new traveler. Porto is a beautiful and quaint city, with walkable streets in the city center, a Riverwalk a few blocks of rolling hills away, and a beach a quick train ride from our apartments. On the flip side, Portuguese isn't a very common language, and it's less like Spanish than I had anticipated. It also doesn't have the infrastructure that other places in Europe have, so it's a little more work to pay with a credit card or find people who speak English. For the first couple of weeks, I didn't venture out much; I was still timid with the public transportation and the language barrier. Not that this is news; even at home, I don't walk around making eye contact or talking to strangers. As I wandered the streets silently, taking in the unique architecture and occasional street murals, I seemed to always be searching for potential places to eat. Storefronts and delis boasted Jamón, which is dry-cured like what you might find on a charcuterie board, not the ham you pick up at Honeybaked Ham for Thanksgiving dinner, dangling from the ceilings and attracting what seemed to me an unsanitary number of flies. This was in stark contrast to the stores and restaurants in the U.S., where the food laws are too strict to allow hunks of uncovered meat to dangle for an extended amount of time anywhere other than a subzero freezer.

    Thankfully, I stumbled across two coffee shops that became my home away from home. They keep me caffeinated and lightly fed with gourmet-looking avocado toast, which I don't think I had ever consumed prior to this trip. Dinners were a bit more stressful since they fell smack in the middle of my workday, which was still 8 am 5 pm U.S. Pacific time zone. Secondarily, there seemed to be an abundance of local food focused heavily on meat, and not just the hunks of jamón were peering at me through the glass of the deli windows on every corner. Listen, it's not like I'd been brainwashed by our food laws in the Americas. My cynicism runs deep enough that I do question food laws that allow fast food pink slime to masquerade as a hamburger but don't allow fresh meat that came straight from an animal to hang from a storefront. Anyway, people rave about how great the jamón is, but I'm not big on the texture of meat. That's okay; I was carrying around all that extra weight, so skipping a couple of dinners wasn't going to kill me.

Upon arrival in this new time zone, my body soaked up the ability to sleep late into the morning. Since I was working U.S. hours, I didn't have to set an alarm clock to be ready for work in the late afternoon. Instead, I allowed my body to determine when it had rested enough. For the first week, I rolled into the coworking space around noon, which was 4 am at home in the U.S. I'd check LinkedIn and send out a few messages to get a head start on my day, then roll out to walk around the beautiful city for a while until I had to start work, around 4 pm Portugal time. This turned out to be one of the biggest blessings of traveling in a different time zone; sleep and the repair my body so desperately needed were now easily obtainable. No jarring alarm clock sending my adrenals into overload before dawn.

June in Porto was a very comfortable temperature, and it allowed me to sleep with the French doors open onto the cute little balcony overlooking the historic street I lived on. Some mornings, I would regret that decision as the downtown neighborhood woke up and became lively on the street below. However, this gently became my new alarm clock, a more soothing version of my chaotic mornings at home. If I wanted to sleep more, I would close the doors and draw the shades. However, I was surprised by how quickly my body adjusted and naturally came alive at a reasonable hour, ready for an espresso and the newness of everything around me each day.

As I walked around the city, taking in the sights during the day, nearly every breath I took was full of secondhand smoke. I quickly realized the Portuguese apparently didn't get the Surgeon General's warning that smoking is harmful to your health. Is there a polite way to walk around town plugging your nose? I decided probably not, so instead, I walked and silently choked down tobacco clouds. Arizona had passed smoking laws years prior that banned smoking in public places, and I had taken them for granted, a fact of which I had become acutely aware.

Any time I'm exposed to a significant amount of smoke, I come down with a sinus infection. I found that it was no different in Porto, and it landed me in bed for a couple of days during my second week. As much as I wanted to lay in bed with my French doors open to enjoy the glorious weather while recovering, the neighbor above me was enjoying the cool breeze by chain-smoking on the balcony. Suddenly, a clatter on my patio disturbed my rest and piqued my curiosity as to the source. It wasn't a large patio and wasn't accessible from the street, so I couldn't fathom what could have caused the clanking noise. When I inspected the balcony, I noticed a cigarette lighter lying on the floor. I immediately picked up the lighter and chucked it over the edge onto the street. Logic told me anyone smoking 86 cigarettes in a row probably has a backup lighter, but my immature passive aggressiveness still made me feel slightly better. Moments later, I heard a knock on my door, and it turned out that the neighbor above was looking for their lighter. Oops, I'd never been so glad not to speak Portuguese! I slinked back to my room and shut the patio doors so I could rest up and get back to exploring my new city.

My second observation, or more of a realization, was that I grew up surrounded by absolutely zero culture or history. Seriously, in Arizona, most of the buildings are cheap stucco squares that were thrown together over the last 50 years and designed to all look the same. Big corporate homebuilders churn these babies out as quickly as transplants from the overpriced California market can buy them. But there in Porto, shit was old. The buildings have intricate detail and a history behind the architect who designed them hundreds of years ago or artists who ordained them with beauty. Raw materials were fit together with precision, and stained glass or uniform carvings in stone made me wonder how these structures were ever created with the limited technology that existed at the time of construction. It provided a sense of awe that I didn't even realize was missing in my life. I've never once walked around

Phoenix, Arizona, in awe of anything, except maybe the days when temperatures were over 120 degrees, and we were in awe that our thighs didn't melt into the seat of the car. Appreciating amazing architecture and artistic detail was a far more enjoyable experience.

As I planned for my trip and imagined what Porto would be like, I had pictured this seaside town where I'd spend a ton of time on the beach. Peering at Google Maps, I imagined walking to the shore, which was only a tiny blip away from my apartment on the screen. Of course, in real life, that was around five miles distance, much too far to walk in a reasonable amount of time. The idea of trying to call an Uber or hop on a train, with my little understanding of the Portuguese spoken around me, gave me angina. My introverted self settled for walking up and down all the streets within a mile radius of my apartment. Alone, I meandered by old buildings and churches, ducked into coffee shops, and maybe read an occasional plaque with historical facts listed rather than signing up for a group tour that would require interaction with strangers. Besides, my short-term memory sucks, so I knew I wouldn't remember any of the historical facts anyway. Oh, and I took a ton of pictures, lots and lots of pictures. It might sound like I was missing out on something, not really interacting with people, but I didn't feel like I was missing anything. It was my slightly socially awkward way of introducing myself to Europe.

Wine Tasting

A few weeks into the Porto trip, Grace, my new 30-something friend from Texas, invited my roommate and me to take a day trip to wine country with her and her roommate. I'd been spending more time with Grace after I met her at that first group dinner and was drawn to her energy, as well as some of her viewpoints about health. Natural health had been kind of a side passion of mine for a long time, and Grace was this kind of free-spirit, yogi type, who seemed like the embodiment of that belief system. Grace's roommate, Emma, was a British girl still in her early twenties, one of the youngest in our group. Funny, because she was light years more mature than most group members, myself included. I guess you shouldn't judge a book by it's…age.

Emma also turned out to be a masterful planner and an experienced traveler. She had been everywhere. On the quieter side, she surprised me with how she navigated herself through new experiences with the ease and confidence of an old soul. She did all the legwork to plan this outing to Douro Valley, a lovely day trip from Porto to the region producing port wine. I was so grateful because just arriving at the Porto train station was overwhelming. I'd never been on a train before, so I was unfamiliar with the whole process. Would we have to go through security? Were we supposed to arrive a certain amount of time before departure, like an airport?

How would we find the right train? Would we need identification? I was rushing my roommate through her cappuccino order, worrying about these details, so we arrived a bit cranky without our usual breakfast.

It turned out we didn't allow ourselves enough time, especially considering the magnitude of the Porto train station. It wasn't large like an airport, but it was old and clearly full of historical architecture. Tile murals were everywhere in Portugal, and the train station was no exception. It was utterly photo-worthy, but we didn't have time to stop and truly take it all in. Emma was texting us to hurry up, and we finally caught up with her and Grace on the platform.

The train ride was the first time I remember getting to sit down and get to know Emma. I enjoyed talking to her, though I think I probably irritated the fuck out of her with my vocal complaints about the weather once we arrived in Douro Valley. First, let me tell you that on this particular day, it happened to be a nice balmy 107 degrees Fahrenheit along the Douro River.

WTF? I am from Phoenix and I thought it was hot as balls.

Color me stupid, but I had always thought wine was grown in cooler regions. Being from Arizona, I grew up thinking about wine coming from Napa Valley or Washington state, which are considerably cooler climates than the Phoenix like temperatures in the Douro Valley. As soon as we hopped off the train at the Pinhao stop, we were surrounded by the cutest photo-worthy building, with tile murals reflecting the vineyards in mosaics of blue and gold all around the middle section of the exterior walls. More overpowering than the awe of such a decorative public transportation building was the dry, crisp heat we were hit with upon exiting. Any wind that happened to blow through felt as if you were squaring off with a blow dryer.

We escaped the heat by touring the lovely Quinta do Bomfim vineyards, which was only a quick walk along brick streets lined with bougainvillea. Emma, our superstar planner, had thought ahead and booked a picnic onsite at the vineyard. We were all ravenous after almost no breakfast and a two-hour train ride. Her foresight and the lunch both proved to be stellar. Excellent service from the vineyard staff and our lunch was cute servings of yumminess packed in glass mason jars like little gifts...it was setting up the 2nd vineyard for failure, but they didn't have to accept the task with such open arms. So, we felt good, with our tummies full and a couple of glasses of wine sampled before we took off across the Douro River to the next vineyard. The short walk across the bridge felt something like the Murph workout in CrossFit. I jest, sort of. So, we arrived for our next wine tour, a bit sweaty and needing some air conditioning.

We entered Quinta das Carvalhas' stately reception room with nice heavy furniture, a detailed wood-worked bar, and expensive bottles of wine on display. That was about where the niceties ended, with the inanimate objects. The sour woman at the desk barely spoke to us. Nobody showed us where to go or announced that the tour was leaving; I had to gather our group so we wouldn't miss the bus. We were promised a scenic drive up hills of vineyards to get a spectacular view of the river and vineyards.

Sounded great, in theory. Did I mention it was 107 degrees?

We all piled onto this minibus: our group of four and a French couple. Our guide was a delightful college student practicing her English by giving tours and she was a refreshing contrast from the snarky woman working at the front desk. There we are on the bus. Driving up the winding road. With the sun beating down on the side of the hill. With no air conditioning. And no water. Meanwhile, I was praying for sweet death to remove me from my discomfort.

Then, we stopped, YAY! Oh shit, it was only because we were stopping at various points to learn about cool vineyard shit. Standing in the sun. On the hill. With no water. Waiting to get back on the bus with no air.

We slowly made our way to the top, and I made out less and less of what the tour guide was saying. I was fading.

I just wanted to get in the bus and floor it to the top of the hill so I could hurtle myself from the top of wherever we were going. *Okay, a bit dramatic, but you have to feel our pain....IT WAS SO HOT!*

Fast forward, we finished the bus tour, and nobody died, so we went back to the reception area for wine tasting. Except by this point, nobody gave a shit about wine. We were all red-faced, sweaty, almost comatose, and practically begging for water. We were met with a huff from the belligerent lady in the reception area and then were each charged grandly per water.

So apparently, we could have service with a smile for wine (kidding, she never smiled), but some serious attitude for water, the fluid we need to survive? *Um, can I trade my wine for water? Yes, I do realize that is a twist on some Bible shit.* Once our core body temperature cooled below 100 million degrees, we awkwardly left the building under the disapproving glare of the aforementioned lady, never to return, and we all lived happily ever after. The End.

Moral of the story: Don't visit Quinta das Carvalhas if ever in Douro Valley, Portugal. Second moral of the story: Something wonderful happened that day. First, I (the one who barely likes people) bonded with three women I hardly knew prior to this trip. Second, the experience of buying a train ticket, learning how the train station worked, finding my stop, navigating a new location and getting back to the original destination is extremely liberating. This experience boosted my confidence exponentially, and I was ready to try another something I'd never done before: travel to a new country totally by myself.

♥

Vigo

Following the liberating wine tour, I immediately summoned enough courage to book a train ticket for a solo trip to Vigo, Spain, before I could wuss out. Ah, España.

Although it was the next country on our itinerary, and I was already slated to spend a month in Valencia a few short weeks later, I couldn't wait to visit *the promised land*. Vigo is on the Western shoreline on the opposite side of the country as Valencia, so I figured it would be nice to see as much of the country as possible. There are certain milestones in life where you believe you have passed into a new realm of adulthood. At 16, you feel so mature as you taste your first sip of freedom by obtaining a driver's license. Perhaps some revisit this again at 18, being able to vote. (Since I hold a high level of disdain for politics, I'm just guessing on this one.)

Becoming a parent and being responsible for the life of a human really sobers you into adulthood as well, served with a side of complete panic. Traveling alone internationally proved to be another milestone, marking my entrance into adulthood. Yes, I was 42 years old; I should've already felt like an adult. Hell, my own kid was already an adult. All I have to say is that maturing doesn't always happen in a straight line, continuing on an upward trajectory.

On Friday morning, I was back at the beautiful Porto train station well in advance of my train's departure time. After taking in the murals and architecture of the station, I nervously boarded the rickety old Portuguese train with my overnight bag, laptop, and about $40 worth of Euros in my pocket. My plan was to arrive in Vigo around noon, check into the hotel, do a quick walking tour to acquaint myself, and then back to the hotel to start my work day around 4:00 pm. As I watched the terrain of Portugal fall away outside the window, I was filled with excitement. This had been my dream since Spanish class in junior high, and here it is, the moment I'd waited and wished for. My heart was filled with gratitude and I found myself surprisingly emotional.

One of the tricks to traveling without an international calling plan I learned was to download an offline Google map. Doing this allowed me to follow my 'blue dot' as the train chugged us closer to Spain, even without having a local SIM card or Wi-Fi. Perhaps I thought I would change into some Spanish version of Cinderella once I crossed the border, but I was disappointed when my blue dot crossed the line on the map, and there I was, the same old person I was 7 seconds ago. Damn it. I thought I would feel *different*. But alas, I crossed this imaginary line someone arbitrarily drew on a map as the same old, slightly broken person I previously was. Nothing magical happened. No fairy tale ending. No prince charming arrived to sweep me off to a castle nestled in Northern Spain.

Change is a funny thing. You don't feel it when it's happening because it isn't instantaneous. How could I set off on this journey, not simply to Vigo, but packing up and leaving my home without changing? Yet, in the moment, I didn't feel any different. Was I expecting to be suddenly confident? Or perhaps I would morph from an introvert into an extrovert? Whatever I expected change to feel like, it didn't.

The train ride was too short to process all of my disappointment over not becoming a noticeably different person. When I got off at my stop in Vigo, I began my new journey by walking in the wrong direction to the hotel. After checking Google Maps and my trusty blue dot, I turned and backtracked in the correct direction. Maybe that was a metaphor for life that I missed in the moment; *heading in the wrong direction isn't necessarily bad, so long as you can course correct.* Since I had a few hours until I needed to log onto my computer, I took my time walking. Though I couldn't see the ocean yet, there was a slight breeze that kicked up some salt air, and approximately one million seagulls hanging around told me it was nearby. The road led along the waters of Ría de Vigo, and as I weaved my way toward my hotel, one of the many seagulls flying overhead took a massive shit on my arm. Right onto the only jacket I had brought with me for the weekend. Fabulous. Was this a sign of how my entire solo weekend was going to be, I wondered?

As I reached the hotel and entered the crisp, cool lobby, I was greeted by staff who all spoke perfect English. It was still surprising to me how many people spoke English as a second language. Maybe growing up with such close proximity to the Mexican border in a state with rednecks saying things like, "Go back to where you came from" or "Learn to speak English if you want to live here" hadn't prepared me for how the rest of the world operated. It was so refreshing to feel part of a more global community.

After checking in, I set out to pick up some additional cash from a local ATM. My debit card had worked without fail at the ATMs in Portugal, but I couldn't find one that would accept it in Vigo. Had I known it would be an issue, I would have gotten more Euros before I left Portugal since they conveniently use the same currency. Panic started to set in when I realized I basically had forty bucks to last me the whole weekend. How was I going to entertain myself all weekend on $40? The next day I had planned on taking a ferry to the nearby Cíes Islands, which are supposed to have some of the most beautiful beaches in the world. Luckily, I had already booked that trip on my credit card, so my cash was reserved solely for food. My budget would be limited but doable if I spent it carefully.

Aside from my ferry to the islands, the rest of my activities for the weekend were free. With no one else's agenda to worry about, I strolled around at my leisure. There was a beautiful park on a hill overlooking the water, and I spent several hours checking it out. An expanse of green grass overlooked the ocean, peppered with old stone sculptures. Several sightseers walked between structures, taking pictures, and I realized how weird it felt not to be taking photos with any people in them. Even though I had been walking around Porto alone for almost a month, it felt lonely…no, not lonely, but awkward and maybe a little embarrassing to walk around monuments all by myself.

The next morning, I woke early to catch the ferry to the Cíes Islands. It wasn't a long ride and didn't kick up any motion sickness, so I was quite content when we docked. It wasn't what I had imagined at all. After a quick walk along the path around the island, I realized that was all there was to see. I had planned on this occupying my entire day. I was also confused because I was still looking for the amazing beach that was promised online. I had found the beach, but I don't know that I would describe it as one of the *nicest* beaches in the world. It's still a beach, though, so I spent a few hours doing nothing but lying on the sand and letting the sun warm my bones. For some reason, lying on the beach alone made me feel exposed. Beaches were for vacations in my mind, and I always went on vacation with a significant other. My mind flipped back to the vacation I had taken with Tom a few months before we split. Hadn't I spent time on the beach there alone while everyone else was golfing? Yes, I had spent an entire day drinking mojitos by myself and didn't think once about it. So that confirmed it: this stigma about being alone isn't actually about physically sitting alone on this beach; it was the *knowing* that I would go back to my hotel alone, go back to Portugal alone, and eventually go back to the U.S. alone. It was more the uncomfortableness of going through life alone, not the experience on this particular beach in Spain. As it got hot, I realized another challenge of being solo, though it was more superficial. How was I to leave my personal belongings on the beach while I took a dip in the ocean? I was very nervous about leaving my few remaining Euros on land, but finally, the heat won, and I discretely tucked my wallet under the beach towel for a quick reprieve in the waves.

Hunger finally hit me by early afternoon. There were only two spots with food on the island: a little hut overlooking the ocean and a big cafeteria-style building right next to the boat dock. Predictably, I decided to check out the less touristy spot. The menu was completely in Spanish, but not the same dialect of Spanish I had learned as a kid, so it was hard to translate. There was one item that I recognized as being "white fish," so I ordered it. I love tilapia, sea bass, and all the other white fish I've ever had, so it seemed like a safe bet. Wouldn't you know the plate I received was filled with small whole fish, scales, eyeballs, and all. They appeared to resemble a cooked sardine.

How was I even supposed to eat these? I'd never been served bite-sized whole fish before. Should I bite it in half and only eat the tail end, or was the entire head edible? A table nearby had ordered the same thing, so I was trying not to be too obvious as I intently stared when they reached into their basket. It appeared the other table was popping the entire fish into their mouth.

Ugh.

Brains and eyeballs and everything?

Even though I wasn't a fan of sardines, I was starving, and didn't have enough money to order something different. "Is this seriously what I'm about to do right now?" I thought. I held my breath and popped one into my mouth, certain my gag reflex would push the half-eaten carcass out as soon as it hit my tonsils. Surprisingly, the skin was crispy and the only flavor I picked up on was salt. They were like gross-looking fish-shaped protein chips. I polished off the whole basket full, proud that I had the courage to try them.

Before I knew it, my weekend was over, and it was time to head back to Porto. I spent the few remaining Euros on espresso and a croissant at the train station (hint: Don't do this; you never get good coffee and pastries at the train station). The train was late, which made me slightly anxious because I was out of money, but eventually, it rolled into the station. The Spanish trains were much nicer than the Portuguese version that brought me here. As I sunk into the unexpected luxury, I pretended like I belonged here, speeding across the Spanish countryside. Aside from the moment of anxiety when the train was late, and I was out of money, I noticed that I was far more comfortable on my return ride. Perhaps it was due to the nicer accommodations on this train line, or perhaps I'd spent the entire weekend working a muscle I didn't know I had. The *alone* muscle. While my mother frequently reminded me of my toddler days of consistently exclaiming, "I do it MYself!" there was a certain naivety I had carried around with me my whole life. Sure, I could do things by myself in my hometown. But here, I was alone for real, for probably the first time ever. It was like I was meeting myself for the first time, and I was finally comfortable enough to allow for silence in the conversation. I arrived back in Porto in one piece, both excited and reflective to have accomplished my first weekend totally alone in a new country!

♥

Spain

In a flash, my time in Portugal had expired, and I found myself in the airport in Valencia. My roommate from Porto was supposed to also be my roommate in Valencia, but she fell hard for a local guy she met there. She struggled over the decision to move on to the next location or stay and pursue a relationship that was only a few weeks in the making. Much to my surprise, I found myself saying, "You should stay and see where it goes. You never know." And I meant it. I wasn't just giving her lip service while secretly thinking it was the dumbest idea I'd ever heard. I didn't even know I had it in me to believe in following one's heart. Who was I even becoming? A few months ago, if a friend had asked me if they should stay *anywhere* for a guy, I would have said an emphatic, "FUCK NO, guys are assholes; let's go to Spain!" As I thought about her new romantic adventure, it occurred to me that I hadn't met a single good-looking guy the whole time I was in Portugal. Were there truly no handsome men, or had I been so busy focusing on the delight of travel that I temporarily forgot about the distraction of male companionship? Whatever it was, I liked the momentary reprieve from reliving the past or throwing myself into the future. Each day of living was adventure enough in itself.

Spain was the country on the itinerary I was the most obsessed with seeing. Not only because I had wanted to go to Spain since I was a child. Back then, it would have been an immersive experience to help solidify my knowledge of the language, but now it had been so long since Spanish class that I may as well have never even taken it. Since my taste of Spain during my weekend trip to Vigo, which wasn't earth-shattering, I had developed a hope that living in Valencia for a month would be different. I undoubtedly wanted Spain to be as inspiring as I'd imagined for the last thirty years. No pressure, España!

Our digital nomad group split up from the airport as everyone headed to the pre-booked Airbnbs. As everyone gathered to jump into taxis based on their assigned apartment, I found myself alone again. My Porto roommate had stayed behind, and our third roommate for the month was supposed to be a new addition, but she didn't show up. To make it more awkward, my apartment was the only one not ready to be checked into yet. Up until then, I had only stayed in Airbnbs, which are used for rental purposes 100% of the time. But in Valencia, rentals were hard to come by, and I was booked in a family's home while they went on a month holiday. They were still packing and moving out, so I joined Grace's Airbnb group as they checked in to kill time. We entered a historical-looking building and crammed into the tiniest elevator I'd ever seen. It looked like it was straight out of a black-and-white movie. Luckily, the small elevator was deceiving, and we entered a grand apartment that was open and bright, with three spacious bedrooms and an enormous kitchen. It was gorgeous! This surely set me up for disappointment when I finally got to see my new location.

There was a car pulled up outside my apartment building crammed so full of random miscellaneous items that there wasn't a single nook or cranny left. As I walked by to see if a homeless person was living in it, I almost missed the old splendor that was my building. Since the front of the building faced a narrow walkway where buildings were tucked so close side by side that they seemed to share a wall, it was hard to take in the entire building visually. If you stepped all the way to one side, you could look up the stone face and see all the intricate carvings and ornate detail. Giant wooden doors marked the entrance, and above, I could see wrought iron balconies just large enough to take one step out on. Once I lugged my suitcase up to the third-floor apartment, I found the door was open, and a family with two small children was frantically trying to clear haphazardly packed boxes from the flat. It was clear they were ill-prepared and disorganized, so I headed down to a coffee shop around the corner for a cappuccino and a biscuit while I waited for this family to get their shit together (literally and figuratively). Once outside the building, I realized the car was not the temporary home of an unfortunate victim of circumstance but belonged to the family whose apartment I was renting. There was no way they could fit four people in that car. I braced myself for a longer wait than one cappuccino would provide, but I couldn't go far, considering I had my suitcase in tow.

Unfortunately, it was siesta time in Spain. I'd heard about this time of day that was like an extended lunch, but honestly, it seemed like make-believe when hearing about it from home. No U.S. company in their right mind would shut down in the afternoon for a couple of hours. But, when I tried to find an open shop to grab a coffee, I learned it was, in fact, true. I didn't realize how starving I was after the flight until I started wandering the streets pulling a suitcase, peering into storefronts looking for an abierto sign. Finally, I got lucky and found a place open for coffee, but they weren't serving food. Thankfully, in Spanish culture, it's common practice to bring a little treat or biscuit alongside your coffee.

Two coffees and biscuits later, I received the message that I could check in and unpack my bags. Initially, as I walked into the apartment, it appeared dingy and not well organized. Trinkets and tchotchkes were on every surface, the furniture was cheaply constructed, and the couch appeared to have stains in the fabric. A far cry from the grandeur of Grace's place. Since I was staying here alone after losing both my roommates for the month, I had my pick on the three bedrooms. I assumed I'd take over the primary bedroom, but seeing the condition of the room and attached bathroom, I had to rethink. There was dust and dirt everywhere, and the bathroom was disgusting. All the personal toiletries were left as is, stuffed in shower caddies and on every possible surface that could hold another dirty, half-used bottle of something. When I found crumpled-up rags stuffed into the corners of the bathtub ledge, I went into an angry frenzy. Why would anyone rent out their home and leave it in this condition?

There was a child's bedroom with a tiny twin bed and cheap, threadbare sheets, but it seemed to be the cleanest in the home, so I chose it as my home base for the next thirty days. There was no air conditioning in any of the bedrooms, and this window faced the interior courtyard of the building, so I figured there would be less street noise since I had to keep the window open all the time. The heat was stifling in July, so closing the windows was not an option without AC. The apartment was advertised as having air conditioning, but as I searched through all the rooms, I found that it only applied to the one-room unit installed in the living room. If I wanted to sit on the stained couch next to a baby bouncer, I could temporarily receive some relief from the July heat.

Rather than unpack, I decided I would be less creeped out if I left my clothes in my suitcase. In the primary bedroom, I hoisted my bag onto the master bed and opened it fully so both sides of the suitcase could act as makeshift drawers and prevent my clothes from coming in contact with any objects in this filthy house. I found the washing machine in the kitchen and opened it to inspect the condition. As I suspected, there was mold around the rubber ring and it smelled musty as hell. Looks like I'd be using a laundromat all month; I hoped there was one close by. In the kitchen, I noticed the same dirty wash rags piled around the kitchen sink, along with baby bottles turned upside down to dry and an iPhone sitting on the counter. Inside the refrigerator were remnants of old fruit and vegetables that had rotted and stuck to the bottom of the crisping drawers. Though the drawers were emptied, the rot was left behind as a crusty reminder that this was not *my* home.

Why did these people Airbnb their apartment? They were a complete disaster. There's no way I'd ever live like this, much less rent my house for someone else to stay in for a month and then bequeath it to a total stranger in this state of stale disarray. It's gross, but I was also exhausted. Since my check-in was delayed so long waiting for them to get the fuck out of there, I decided to wait until the next day to submit a message to the host to report the condition of the home, as well as the iPhone that was left behind. At that moment, I was tired from the travel and hardly had the energy for anything other than getting some rest.

The tiny twin bed felt like sleeping on a crib mattress. It was so flimsy and squeaked like plastic every time I moved. If I had to guess, I'd say it took me half the night to fall asleep between the chintzy bed and the stifling heat. The open window didn't do much since the open courtyard in the center of the building was surrounded by more…building.

A noise woke me with a start the next morning, far too early for the amount of sleep I'd had, but the sun was already shining in the windows. Early morning disorientation prevented me from immediately recognizing where I was when I opened my eyes, but then I quickly remembered the sad, dirty apartment I had checked into yesterday. As I looked around the room to reorient myself, I saw a small child standing at the door. My heart was pounding as I sat straight up in the bed. "Fucking hell, what is a kid doing in my doorway?" I thought! Rather than fear for my life, I momentarily gave thanks that I don't sleep in the nude.

A female voice came from deeper in the house, saying something in Spanish, and the little girl disappeared. Hesitantly, I got out of bed to follow her down the hall to find out what was going on. As I turned the corner into the kitchen, I saw the homeowner from yesterday standing in the kitchen wearing a baby in a pack on her body. She had a large bag of toilet paper, the iPhone that had been left behind, and a few other random items tucked into any carrying space on her person. Since I couldn't understand what she was saying, and she couldn't understand what I was saying, she motioned to her phone, and I inferred that she came back to get her phone. Rather than yell in a language she didn't understand, I just stood there and looked at her as disapprovingly as I could muster in my surprised state. She hurried her daughter out the door and said something I imagined must be an apology.

My plans then changed from simply reporting the home's condition to reporting the owner re-entering the home without notifying me she was coming or even having the courtesy to knock before she entered. I crafted a detailed message and took pictures of everything from the dirty dishrags to the crusty crisping drawers to back up my complaint. I was leaving Valencia the following day for a little side trip to Ibiza, so I asked for the home to be in livable condition by the time I returned or to find me a different rental for the remainder of the month. One thing was certain: I had no intention of waking up to a little girl standing in the bedroom doorway again. When I left for Ibiza, I took all my personal items with me, just in case the owners decided to come hang out in their house again while I was gone. What a fucking shit show! España and I were not off to a good start.

When I returned, the apartment had been cleaned. The wash rags were gone, and things appeared to have been surface-cleaned at least. It wasn't the type of clean you get from actually taking care of your home every day, but it would suffice enough for me to stay the remainder of the month. I used their mismatched, threadbare, and slightly crusty bath towels to lay over the couch and any other surface I had to sit on. For my own use, I headed to the Zara Home store to buy my own fresh new fluffy towel so I could at least shower.

July in Valencia dragged on at a much slower pace than in Porto. Feasibly, it made sense since it was the second country on the itinerary, and a tiny amount of the novelty of travel had worn off. A larger part of it was probably due to living alone. Even though I'm an introvert and lived alone back home, I missed being able to come home and chat about new restaurants or discoveries with my Porto roomie. I wondered how she was doing with her new boyfriend. I hoped he wouldn't end up being some weird axe murderer after I encouraged her to stay. That would suck.

Why would I even think of him being an axe murderer? I've always had a tendency to think of the most negative outcome in any situation. Over the last month, Grace had already pegged that about me and encouraged me to purchase a black onyx bracelet we found at a vendor stand during one of our first days in Spain. Black onyx, she explained, helps to pull negative energy from our being. I didn't much about crystals and wasn't convinced that one bracelet could help this giant dark cloud that I called my 'personality,' but it was worth a shot. I placed the bracelet on my wrist and didn't take it off.

Grace left Spain after a few days to meet her boyfriend in Italy, and Emma was working non-stop, so I found a local coffee shop to plant myself at every day to work. As much as my apartment sucked, it was in a great part of town. My 10-minute walk to the coffee shop wound me past beautiful museums and churches and high-end retail shops and landed me in the cutest little café with window seats, like you could literally sit with one leg out the window on the sidewalk and the other inside the café. It was the type of place I could leave my computer at the table while I used the restroom without worrying about anyone running off with my shit. Plus, if I worked long enough, they had a full bar, so you could easily transition from a latte to a Spanish gin and tonic. My visits became longer and longer, as I dreaded spending any more time than I had to in that crappy apartment. When I arrived home after dark, I had to use all my force to open the large, heavy wooden doors into the old building. Electricity must have been invented well after the building was erected, as the light switch was across the foyer and required a few seconds walk in the dark. Not that it was a big deal, except for the giant sewer roach always inside the doorway to greet me. I named him Juan Pablo, and upon entering in the dark, I would shuffle my flip-flops across the marble floor to avoid crunching him under my feet. Perhaps I was beginning to lose my sanity, like Tom Hanks in *Castaway*. If he could talk to a volleyball, I could name a cucaracha.

    I spent some of my stifling hot, late nights on the phone with friends back home since I was not sleeping anyway. It provided a certain sense of connection and comfort and, more importantly, a distraction from this feeling of aloneness and a pull to turn the microscope inward. My thoughts had continued to return to my past and how I ended up in this unusual position. While I had never believed much in religion, spirituality, or whatever, I always believed that everything happens for a reason. I would use a left-brained approach to analyze the situation and figure out what lesson I was supposed to learn from it. My more cynical side told me the lesson was to never trust men. Hadn't I learned that early in life? As much as I tried to stuff it down, my mind would return to elementary school and the man my mother met at church and eventually married. Before he entered our life, we were young and carefree kids. We knew we didn't have much because our friends all had things we couldn't afford, but otherwise, we were pretty happy. Though divorced, our parents co-parented and we always felt loved and as though they gave us as much as they could. But that all changed when we got our new "stepdad." He was jealous and didn't like my dad stopping by after we got home from school, so my dad's visits had to be scheduled. We tried to be understanding because this new man in our life was, for one, new. He was from the church, and was also disabled with MS. He could still walk using crutches, but he mostly lived sitting in his recliner in front of the TV set. Prior to him entering our lives, we couldn't afford cable television, but now we had a big brown cable box sitting on top of the bulky TV. Sometimes he would ask us to change the channel for him to save the awkward stumbling that was required since the disease had ravaged his nervous system's communication with his legs. I remember being caught in a conundrum as a child, wanting to be helpful but conversely wanting to avoid ever being in close proximity to this man. I had learned to dread hearing the phone ring. Back in the 1980s, phones weren't pocket-sized computers. Our house had one telephone, an ugly beige color, affixed to the wall between the kitchen and dining room. It had a long curly cord between the base and the receiver, so it could reach several feet in any direction, giving a little freedom to walk around and still be on the phone (being mobile while on the phone in those days was a luxury).

As a small child, it was fun to stretch the cord as far as it could go, then wrap it around my body like a mummy, each turn taking me closer to the receiver fixed on the wall. By the time I was in fifth grade, that activity was no longer fun. When the phone rang, it required walking within proximity of my stepdad's chair. Even trying to take as wide a berth as possible would still put you right on the fingertips edge of his wingspan. If the timing was unlucky for me, he would reach out after I answered the phone and pull me in his lap. To the untrained eye, an observer might think it was sweet that this man was trying to bond. As his stepdaughter, I knew it meant only one thing: at least one hand would be waiting for me, palm upturned and perfectly placed underneath my buttocks. He never told me not to tell anyone about his fondling; he just took advantage of the innocence of youth and the nature of children to assume that anything bad that was happening was of their own doing. Inside, I knew it was wrong. I knew it made me feel yucky, and I wanted to avoid him. It also made me feel like I wasn't safe in my own home, this place where we were perfectly happy, albeit a little poorer, before he came along. The thought never even crossed my mind that I should tell my mom or dad about what was happening. Inside, hate started growing.

I hated this man.

I hated being around him and pretending he wasn't a creep.

I hated going to church and seeing him praised for being a family man and a stellar example for the disabled community.

I hated being at home.

Once I was out of elementary school, the opportunities for him to act on these impulses must have come in more short supply. I started spending the night at friends' homes as often as I could, sometimes making excuses not to go home all weekend. By the time high school hit, my mom had divorced him, never knowing the full level of damage he had already done.

That hate was something I carried around for years and directed toward most men. Isn't it funny how biased we are for the negative? I had so many examples of wonderful men; my dad, my grandpa, my brother, my uncles, and so many more were positive reflections of what the gender was capable of being. But what had stuck with me was this one blip of ugly in my life, making me resentful, untrusting, angry, and afraid of speaking my truth. The other interesting thing it made me feel was weak. Both weak for not feeling able to control my circumstances as a child, but also weak because I knew that many young girls experienced a much worse fate at the hands of perverts. Why should I be so damaged over a little inappropriate fondling? Couldn't it have been so much worse? Why wasn't I stronger and less affected by this?

Building walls was a solution to help me feel stronger. If I kept people out, they couldn't hurt me. Hadn't that served me over the years? As I was sitting there pondering, the black onyx bracelet that Grace had encouraged me to buy, broke. Little black round beads started hitting the dirty apartment floor and rolling in every direction. Scrambling to catch them all pulled me back into the reality of my dingy little lonely apartment. This place was so depressing and dark, it was almost hard to breathe with all the negativity vibrating in between those walls. Even though I felt like I had toured every old church around, I suddenly had to leave this place and go walk through another gothic creation to clear my juju.

When Grace heard about the bracelet, she laughed about how full of negative energy I was. She said the bracelet broke because you're supposed to take the crystals off and 'charge' them to release the negative energy. You can do this by placing them in moonlight, sunlight, or running them under clean water. I'd never heard of such a thing and I was reluctant to believe it, but it did track with all the negative memories that I had time to ponder over the month, but that wasn't a detail I had shared with Grace. Thankfully, she would be returning soon from Italy, and I hoped she was ready for a new bestie because I needed a strong drink and some girl talk!

♥

More Wine Tasting

Grace finally returned and I was so excited to meet up to hear about her trip to Italy over gin and tonics. Funny, I never had a G&T prior to going to Spain. It's not really a Spanish drink, but they have a special way of serving it that makes it absolutely delish. First, they start with an oversized wine glass or goblet which allows for a lot of ice. Letting the liquid flow through all the ice in such a large glass changes the flavor in a magical way. My favorite G&T bar in Valencia had a million options on the menu, depending on your preference of gin and garnish. I preferred it with either citrus or elderberries (or both), and it quickly became my new favorite drink. Grace was happy to join me while she recounted all the interesting places she visited in Italy.

Emma had been researching wine tours in the few moments she didn't spend working and was ready to plan an excursion for us. Shocking, I know…more wine. Since my Porto roommate didn't come to Spain, it was just the three of us this time. None of us had picked up any new friends, even though a few additional digital nomads joined the group for the month in Spain. Most of the new nomads fit in with the twenty-something group, who were more interested in touristy trips or partying. While I didn't expect to make many friends during my travel, I noticed myself getting a little judgy of the younger group. Not like it was their fault they had nothing in common with a slightly overweight, cynical, empty nester, forty-something. I could have been their mother.

Anyway, Emma hit a home run with this private wine tour she found out of Valencia. We started off on a Sunday morning with our tour guide, a crotchety old Irish guy. He picked us up to drive us about an hour outside of town to the Chozas Carrascal vineyard. We weren't in the car for two minutes when he announced that the vineyard charged extra because it was a Sunday, so we would have to pay an extra 20 euros if we still wanted to go. Mind you, he had already started driving toward the vineyard. Basically, pay up or get the fuck out.

Okaaay, well, we are in the car...and driving...so I guess we will pay???

And off we went on our little drive. Along the way he entertained us with all the things that piss him off. To summarize with the CliffsNotes version: everyone is shit, everything is shit. It might sound awful, but in fact, it was hysterical. This was my kind of tour!

Between the tirades about everything sucking, he in effect shared quite a bit of information. He was super knowledgeable about a wide range of topics, so he peppered us with a ton of facts about Spain (and other regions), delivered with his salty attitude. And let me tell you, the guy knew his wine backward and forward. He was so detailed and set up quite the tasting at the vineyard for us. He did such a great job pairing the foods and the wines that we were a bit buzzed by the end of the day.

During the pouring of the reds, he went on a rant about the temperature of red wine and that all the restaurants in Spain were shit and the idiots running them couldn't properly serve a glass of wine if their life depended on it. Naturally, we asked him for a recommendation on where to go in Valencia if we wanted to drink wine *properly*. According to our angry Irish sommelier (he was warming up to us now....or maybe we were drunk, so that's what we thought), there was only one wine bar to go to.

Fast forward to the following weekend. We decided to try said recommended bar. After dinner on Saturday night, we headed to the wine bar. Since dinner in Spain began around 9 pm, we arrived at the wine bar around midnight. We sat outside the last open table and waited for the wait staff. Given our experience in Valencia, we didn't expect anyone to be extraordinarily friendly. Our waitress went beyond our expectation of 'not friendly'; she was downright pissed off that we were there. We politely asked for a menu en Español, and after rolling her eyes at us, she said something rapid-fire in Spanish that none of us could understand.

She huffed inside, got us a menu, and proceeded to tell us that the bar closed at 1:30 am so we were too late to order any food. Since it was only 12:10 am, we had figured that we would have plenty of time for a glass of wine and dessert. Apparently, we figured incorrectly. She took pride and spoke slow deliberate Spanish when she told us we could only order wine from the open bottles and the only dessert available was cookies. It brought her joy to give us bad news, like when you are at the airport and they get to charge you overage fees on your baggage, all the while smirking at your misfortune.

Our waitress disappeared inside and reappeared with a lukewarm white wine for me and a very cold red for Emma. *Hmmmm, I was no sommelier, but something's amiss.* Being the classy lady that I was, I tried to chug down my white before it got any warmer while Emma was warming her glass of red with both hands wrapped around it. The waitress reappeared with our dessert. A plastic tray of cookies. Not a lovely assortment arranged on a restaurant serving tray…a plastic tray that came straight out of a box of cookies from the convenience mart and plopped them on our table.

A plastic fucking tray. Seriously?

Okay, I admit that one time I had to contribute Rice Krispy treats to my daughter's preschool fundraiser, and I went to Costco and bought a box of individually wrapped treats, cut the wrappers off, and put them on a platter like they were homemade. But everyone knew I didn't make perfectly shaped Rice Krispy treats. At least I had the decency to put them on a platter.

Nope, the wine bitch couldn't be bothered with a plate. Actually, that is a lie; she put the plastic packaging on a plate. Eat from the package like the disgusting American animals that you are. And this was at the *best* wine bar in town? Now I understood why the angry Irish man was so angry. We were taken aback, but honestly, we found it so hysterical we couldn't stop laughing.

♥

Reflections

Expectations can be a bitch. Had I not wanted to travel to Spain since I was a child, I probably wouldn't have been so harsh on the past month. Porto had turned out better than I expected, which probably had something to do with the fact that I expected *nothing*.

But Spain.

I had pictured Spain for so many years in my head, which was silly because it's a whole country, and I had only one vision as if the entire country could be captured in a single Polaroid. Surely I didn't expect an entire country to look like the one picture I had in my head. As illogical as it sounds, I kind of did. During the past month, I'd spent most of my time in Valencia but I also visited Barcelona,

Ibiza, and Cordoba. None of them were what I had in mind, but Cordoba was probably the closest. After taking a weekend trip there, I learned that Seville and some of the towns further south from our Valencia location were most likely the regions I would enjoy. Perhaps I had once seen a photo of Moorish-influenced architecture, which forever stuck in my mind as 'Spanish.'

Valencia and Barcelona had Gothic-style buildings, surrounded by much more modern structures that were erected to handle the sheer number of people who now reside in these metropolitan areas. The South, I was promised, was less of this. There wasn't enough time during this trip to investigate this information for accuracy, so I would have to schedule another trip someday. July had started with so much energy and expectation, but a few weeks in, it had fizzled out. In some ways, the experience was no different than my career, my health, my weight, and my relationships. There were definitely some parallels that a more enlightened version of myself might have noticed, but I don't think I was quite ready for that yet. On one hand, it was a little disappointing that I hadn't experienced Spain the way I thought I would, but it also gave me a reason to come back. Next time, I would book my trip further south. Perhaps I would even take the entire three months of travel allowed on my visa to explore Spain and give it the proper attention it deserved.

My month in Spain, coming to a close, turned out to be a relief. The temperatures were record highs that summer, and with no AC in my bedroom, I spent my nights tossing and turning, trying to find some level of comfort on the scratchy, dry sheets and thin mattress. My legs had been swelling, and some nights, I laid on my back with my legs resting straight up along the wall. Between the lack of cleanliness and the heat, I was hoping this was going to be the worst location of the summer.

We were heading to Prague next, which I heard was also having record heat, but at least their highs appeared to be about 10 degrees cooler. Plus, I found out that Grace, Emma, and I would be sharing an apartment in Prague, so that already sounded better than sitting alone in this shithole. I woke up early on my final day and packed carefully but quickly. I'd straightened the entire house, not that it was ever not neat with me living there, and there was certainly nothing I could do or wanted to do to help the slobs that lived here full time. Instead, I ensured there was no evidence that I'd even been there for the past month other than to leave it slightly cleaner than it was when the crazy owner dropped in to pick up her phone and toilet paper. As I locked the door and took one last look, I felt the burden of this dirty, hot apartment lift off my shoulders. 'Uncomfortable' is the word that comes to mind when describing my stay. Not only the physical nuances of the space but the aloneness. Trying to entertain myself without TV, without friends, and without a community that spoke the same language left me with not much else but to look inside myself.

This was a level of introspection that I wasn't yet ready for. There were still too many feelings stuffed down and demons I was not ready to deal with yet. Suffice it to say, as excited as I was to come to España, I was equally excited to leave.

♥

Prague

Zizkov TV Tower was visible from the living room window in our Prague apartment. We were on the third floor overlooking a park in the Vinohrady neighborhood of Prague, which was an adorable line of communist-style buildings painted in different colors to appear unique despite the uniformity of their architecture. Our building was yellow, one of my favorite colors!

Anyway, the Zizkov Tower was one of the first things we noticed upon arrival. It's hard not to notice because it's so creepy. You might wonder, how can a TV tower possibly be creepy? This particular structure was erected in the country's last year of communism and was voted the second-ugliest building in the world. (I was unaware there was a vote on these things, but the internet yields much in the way of useless information.) In the midst of the beautiful Czech hodge-podge of Romanesque, Gothic, and Renaissance architecture stands a structure taller than the rest. The futuristic design of the tower clashed with everything around it and reminded me of space movies from the 1960s. In 2000, David Cerny designed some faceless baby sculptures, which were affixed to the tower to provide 'warmth.' I'm not sure what his definition of warmth was, but it's definitely different than mine. If you have to affix weird, faceless babies to warm something up, it means it's pretty fucking awful in the first place.

Other than the faceless babies out the window, our apartment was in the perfect location. Right around the corner was the best craft beer bar, The Beer Geek, and it quickly became our favorite place in town. It was underground and dark, with cozy tables squeezed in along its L shape. The current taps were written on a chalkboard, and obtaining a beer usually involved standing three deep in line in front of the chalkboard that spewed facts about IBUs and alcohol content.

It was here one day that Emma and I agreed to a pact. This would be the month we would go out on dates, yes - like the kind involving men. Grace's boyfriend was coming to meet up with her this month, and I suppose we felt a little more adventurous during our third month of travel. We both signed up on dating apps and started the endless swiping through men's faces. Maybe I was too old or too cynical to appreciate this concept, but to save my life, I couldn't find anyone of interest. Photo versions of pissing contests were not my cup of tea. How was I supposed to make a decision based on information as superficial as this? My past wasn't quite 'past' enough for me to feel open to go out with someone without a comprehensive background investigation. However, I persisted only because I made a pact. After filtering potential dates based on my criteria, there were only about five choices. And none of them answered my messages. Maybe that was a blessing in disguise.

Grace was a marketing executive, so she offered to help me create a winning profile and craft my initial messages since my conversion rate was currently 0%. She reviewed my written profile, and the look on her face was a mixture of shock, pity, and surprise.

About Me:
Sarcastic, witty, sometimes funny. I act like I don't care, but I actually do. I hate small talk, so I essentially dread the first date. It's nothing personal. If you send me a dick pic, I will ghost you. Your penis is not the Mona Lisa, no matter what your mama told you. I am not even really sure I should be dating, based on the last few sentences. I might just be having a mid-life crisis. Or indigestion.

The best place to go:
Another country. Or a craft beer bar. I like a good porter or stout. I think IPAs are the devil.

I spend my free time doing:
Traveling, drinking beer, figuring out new ways to offend the human race. I am basically a dude on the inside. No, this isn't code for 'I am actually a man.' I was born a woman and still have all my parts. I just think like a man, allegedly. I have never been one, so this is still unconfirmed.

Grace was kind enough not to immediately delete the entire profile and instead asked, "Why did you choose the most unflattering pictures of yourself?" Apparently, no one on dating sites had heard the phrase, under-promise and over-deliver. "Because that is what I look like in person, so I don't want them to have high expectations and then be disappointed," I replied. Clearly, I should be awarded the title 'worst sales person of all time.' I saw her die a little inside...this wasn't supposed to be such a challenge. She selected new photos and updated my profile, then asked what filters I had set for my search. They all seemed reasonable to me: speak English, have a professional career, and must be between 40 and 55 years old. "You are filtering out all the good ones under 40," Grace told me matter-of-factly. Apparently, I also needed to be more open-minded on age. Yuck, I don't want to date someone younger, especially when men seem to mature more slowly anyway. Grace shook her head and asked, "Why do you have *so many rules*?" Emma chimed in in agreement, "You do make a lot of rules for yourself. You're making this more difficult than it needs to be." I'd never thought of it that way, but I'd always had a certain code of conduct for nearly everything I did. If my life was difficult, at least half of it was self-imposed due to how I think things *have* to be done.

    Of course, Emma almost immediately connected with a guy who seemed to be a perfect fit for her. They were texting via the app and having hilarious conversations, which led to fun in-person dates (per her recount...I wasn't there spying on them). Too bad we were only traveling through for a month, because I could picture them dating.

A bit discouraged by the whole process, I deleted the dating app from my phone and withdrew myself from the 'this will be our dating month' challenge. Part of me was relieved, but another small part felt like a quitter. Until one evening while we were hanging out in the Beer Geek, Grace's boyfriend struck up a conversation with a good-looking guy in line at the chalkboard. In addition to his muscular body, I noticed that his English was excellent. Later, we found out he was an American attending medical school in Prague. Okay, muscular was kind of my thing, but so was smart. Often, you don't get both of those wrapped up in the same package. No offense, meatheads; you guys aren't stereotyped for your IQ. We all ended up sharing a table since the bar was so packed and by the end of the night, I got his WhatsApp number. Perhaps my side of the pact wasn't broken after all.

Funny, before I signed up to travel with this group and found out we would be spending a month in Prague, I had never given this city much thought. For some reason, I had a preconceived notion that Prague would be ugly and boring. It was neither, and it quickly ranked as the favorite city I had visited thus far. There were parks, colorful buildings, castles, a river, and… beer.

So much beer.

Beer gardens were something I decided the United States desperately needed more of. Large open spaces, with green grass and the shade of tall trees, peppered with picnic tables and kiosks selling beer, pretzels, and sausages. Often I would find myself starting my workday here, in the late afternoon Czech sunshine. Beer makes me hate people less, so I'd say it was the perfect way to start a workday where I literally had to talk to people all day (or evening local time). Not like I would get shitty and pass out, but leisurely enjoying a few lagers while the sun went down did wonders to take the stress away. Then, as night would fall in Europe, I would make my way back to the apartment by dinnertime to set up office in my bedroom. There was a small desk I could work from, but usually, I'd lay in bed with my laptop and headphones and work late into the night. Thank a god I don't believe in that Zoom wasn't popular back then, and my calls were either voice or Skype with no video. Emma was usually on calls all day for work, and Grace was always hosting Facebook 'lives' or filming videos, so it worked out best for each of us to be in our respective nooks. We made our eclectic apartment work, even though it only had one bathroom. It beat the hell out of my former life at home, living off Starbucks while chained to an office all day.

    We went on walking tours and food tours, and yes, Emma and I both went out on dates as we promised in our pact. Mine was no love connection, but I felt good that I left my comfort zone for a minute and put myself out there. Plus, it meant I wasn't a quitter. On the other hand, Emma had really taken to her new beau, and he to her. They seemed to be enjoying the process of getting to know each other and had even planned a little weekend getaway to explore a nearby town. With Grace and Emma occupied with their men, I once again found myself reflecting on my failed love life. Instead of allowing myself to be present and feel the pain or loneliness, I pushed the thoughts from my mind. Both literally and figuratively, I stuffed them down with delicious coffee and avocado bread from the cute café across the street from the park. When it became too late in the afternoon for coffee, I replaced it, of course, with beer. Between the two, I remained sufficiently distracted and numb.

As we inched toward the end of our stay here, one of Emma's friends came for a visit. By this point, Grace's boyfriend had moved along, so she and I made plans to go out on the town by ourselves, something we had yet to do here. There were a few nightclubs down toward the city center, which was super touristy but only about a twenty-minute walk from our apartment. We typically tried to avoid the super touristy areas, as backward as that may sound. If we weren't tourists, then what were we? Given our longer stays in each location, we liked to think of ourselves as foreign visitors living here for a while. "What the hell is the difference?" you're probably wondering. Basically, it gave us a reason to feel superior as we walked from our apartment to local cafés stuffed full of digital nomads like us. The locals probably didn't give a shit what we called ourselves; we were all the same to them.

Grace and I discovered that we both love hip hop, especially '90s hip hop featuring Snoop Dog, Dr. Dre, Biggie, and all the other greats, when we were in Bulgaria for a long weekend. She and I, along with Emma, had taken a beer tour around Sofia, the capital city. The last bar of the night was probably the coolest hip-hop club I'd ever seen. Black walls with giant portraits of all my favorite hip-hop artists, framed in shiny gold molding, and the best mix of danceable rap and hip hop blaring from the enormous DJ stand. Grace and I couldn't stop dancing; by the time we called an Uber, the sun was coming up on the horizon.

Grace and I were excited to go out again and recreate that unexpected find in Bulgaria. We had been shopping at all the fun stores in town and had also picked up some items during our jaunt over to Bulgaria, and we were thrilled to have an opportunity to wear them. We went through all our new items and swapped a few things to wear before deciding to get ready for our first real 'night on the town.'

After three months in Europe with no blow dryer or round brush to straighten my naturally wavy hair, it was overgrown, and the roots were heavy with excess oil. At home, I would blow out my hair every single day to make it shiny and presentable. Since my hair is also thick, it requires about 30 minutes and an ionic blow dryer to

111

reduce the frizz. Needless to say, this is a cumbersome process, and I didn't have room in my overweight luggage to carry all these extra items, so I hadn't blown my hair out since the day I left Arizona. And boy, did it look like it. As we prepared to go out, I was annoyed by the texture and stringiness I couldn't disguise. The top was partially straight and the greasiness made full sections clump together, with the bottom portion curling wildly out of control near the nape of my neck. I couldn't even run my fingers through it; it was so tangled with mineral buildup. Without my usual army of hair tools and makeup, I looked more like a DUI mugshot than an American tourist ready to go out on the town. My body wasn't cooperating either; there were additional pounds attached to my hips, thighs, ass, and even creeping into my formerly small waist and back. None of my clothes fit the same, and getting dressed made me feel more like SpongeBob than anyone remotely attractive (sorry, SpongeBob). But I put a smile on my face and kicked my negative insults down deep into my core.

    We could hear the *unce unce* beat of the music before we could even see the club. As we stepped inside a dark hallway and waited our turn to pay the cover charge to get in, the smell of stale beer overpowered us. Grace and I gave each other a look that said, this place looks absolutely filthy...are we seriously going to *pay them money* to go inside? Grace's extrovertedness had influenced me to be more adventurous than I would be on my own. Let's be honest: if I were alone, I wouldn't have left the house. Before we put too much thought into it, it was our turn to pay the overpriced cover charge. There were multiple levels within the club, with each floor equally as dirty as the last, but each one playing a different genre of music. We decided on level 3, which had a giant, albeit a nasty-ass beer-soaked, dance floor and current hip-hop tunes blasting as drunk kids gyrated to the music.

Had I seen the interior of this place prior to paying the entrance fee, I would have suggested pre-gaming with several shots before we left the apartment. Walking into this place sober was like getting punched in the face. We needed to rectify that, so beers were our first priority. Standing in line, we started people-watching. It was pure entertainment. I'd completely forgotten that I looked like a mugshot as I started dishing out my negative judgments of others.

Even though the music here was good, I couldn't jump right into dancing. In my sober state, I was too self-conscious of my lack of natural rhythm. Dancing is so much fun, but it's not something I do well. We quickly chugged a couple of cheap beers served in plastic cups and started to make our way around the building, observing such an eclectic mix of people along the way. As we stood near the bar across from the dance floor, we saw a kid (well, a kid to us) walking around with a Brazilian flag wrapped around his body. As he approached us, he shared that it was his 25th birthday, which I suppose explains the flag-wearing, although I can't say for sure. He wanted a kiss for his birthday, and since Grace was taken, that left me as the only viable candidate. I figured *what the hell* and kissed him, quickly walking away with Grace as we laughed hysterically at the ridiculousness of a 43-year-old kissing a 25-year-old wearing a flag.

We were still laughing when we reached another bar on the other side of the building and got in line behind a young, handsome black man. We made conversation while waiting for our drinks and found out he was from South Africa. Once his order was completed, he approached me instead of walking away from the bar. "May I kiss you?" he asked in his lovely accent. He looked like such a baby face, and I asked him how old he was. "Twenty-one," he responded, and I couldn't help but chuckle. "Oh my god, my daughter is twenty-one!" I said. Mr. South Africa didn't even skip a beat when he said, "Soooo, is that a no?" Sorry, man, that's a definite no. Why I so dramatically drew the line between kissing a 25-year-old and not kissing a 21-year-old, I have no idea. But it made sense to me while in that state of mind.

We continued to circle the dance floor, not quite working up the courage to walk down the metal stairs that led to the half-submerged pit that served as the dance floor. The music was good, but with so many people hanging along the upstairs railing watching all the dancers from above, it made it a bit more intimidating than losing yourself in a crowd of people. If anything was going to influence me to work up the courage, it would be the good-looking brunette guy with whom I kept making eye contact. Grace also saw him and encouraged me to go down and talk to him. Instead, we circled once more and ran into someone dressed like Prince. Not a prince. The Artist Formerly Known as Prince. With his slight build and Fedora hat, he wasn't a foreboding presence, but he quickly made up for that with his stalkery behavior. He put his arm on us to get us to stop when we tried to pass him. In an effort to be nice, we made small talk for a minute. He kept staring deep into my eyes, and it was creeping me out.

Grace saw the distress signal on my face and pulled me into the restroom and out of his grasp. She was laughing hysterically as she said, "You haven't had this much attention the entire time we've been traveling. What the hell is in the beer at this place? They are on you like flies on shit." It was true; even at the beginning of the trip, when my hair was still somewhat presentable, *not one single person* hit on me. Not that anyone ever hits on me at home, either. I usually blame it on my resting bitch face because that is easier to come to terms with than thinking that there is no one on the planet who is interested in me. But maybe I needed to leave the house with greasy hair more often.

Grace made sure that the coast was clear before we exited. Now we were trying to avoid Prince *and* the Brazilian flag wearer, who were both on the main level of the club. So we determined it was finally time to move to the dance floor. We descended the slippery metal steps, trying to avoid the pooling beer since we were both wearing new shoes. The music here wasn't as good as our gem in Bulgaria. We could dance to it, but we weren't as inspired to stay moving and instead found ourselves alternating between the main floor and the dance floor. I kept passing the brunette guy I had locked eyes with earlier, and it seemed he was doing the same. When I was up, he was down, and vice versa. Finally, we managed to be in the same place and ended up chatting through the basics. He was German, and I could tell he was younger than me. When I asked, he told me he was 35, which was still too young per my *rules*. That night, I threw the rule book out and decided to have a little fun with a 35-year-old…

♥

Croatia

Emma was reserved as we headed to the airport in Prague to catch our flight to Croatia. This town had definitely been amazing, but I'd heard so many good things about Croatia I couldn't understand how anyone could be less than ecstatic to be headed there. Rumor was they had the best beaches and most delicious coffee…two of my favorite things. But Emma was British, so maybe beaches and coffee weren't her favorite thing, I reasoned.

Emma and Grace were sharing an apartment for the month, down the street from a basement apartment that I would be sharing with a newcomer to the group. The newbie is my age, so I looked forward to maybe adding a fourth to our little "mature" friend circle. Grace and Emma got dropped off before me, and Emma was already complaining about everything before her feet even hit the ground. The apartment, the town, all of it. I was baffled but still excited.

Walking down the road to my apartment in Split, I looked toward the ocean, but all I could see was massive stone walls that appeared very old, like fortress walls. I imagined what it must have taken to build these impressive walls back in the day before cranes and modern equipment. The local natives must have been very motivated to protect their city from attackers heading in from the sea. My apartment was located right outside the city walls, which gave me access to the main city streets to catch a taxi, but the close proximity to walk anywhere inside the walls, which are pedestrian only. The original city was built inside the high rock walls facing the ocean. While the city had expanded to include much geography outside the walls, inside, the old town seemed to be where all the tourists wanted to be. This should have been an omen. After months of trying not to live like tourists, we were now sprung right in the epicenter of yacht week in Split. Tourists don't spend much time working, so there aren't any nearby coworking spaces or coffee shops set up for Wi-Fi workers like us. And I don't remember who said the coffee in Croatia was amazing because it was mostly shit. There was one good coffee shop inside the city walls, but of course, it was too tiny to work from. I could get my caffeination to go, but work this month would need to be done from my apartment.

Sure, I'd been doing work from my apartment the past several months, but I always had other options; my favorite coffee shop in Spain, the entire city of Prague was Wi-Fi enabled, so anywhere from the coffee shop to the Beer Geek, to a park bench was all potential workspace. This month, my apartment was a basement, so it was dark and a little depressing. Don't get me wrong; it was cute, modern, and, most importantly, clean. No cucarachas named Juan Pablo greeted me at the front door here. But being mostly underground is not appealing to someone who grew up in the Arizona sunshine. I need sunlight like a vampire needs darkness.

Also, who decided the beaches were amazing? First of all, I never even saw a *real* beach. Am I the only one who thinks a beach should have sand? None of these had anything resembling sand. There were pebbles and rocks but no sand. Plus, the water was frigidly cold. I found myself starting to agree with Emma; this place was not the paradise I thought it would be.

After a week, we all picked up a stomach bug, and Emma decided enough was enough. Remember the awesome guy she was spending time with in Prague? He asked her to return to Prague for the rest of the month to stay with him. Damn, this is the second roomie I'd lost to romance on this trip. Was the pang I was feeling jealousy or just a symptom of our illness that we had deemed

'Krka's Revenge' named after the famous waterfalls we visited last weekend here in Croatia? After a little investigation, we found out that although we were told the water was safe to drink from the tap, visitors to the region often get sick from it. Fuck my life. That would have been nice to know about 10 days prior.

The steady stream of diarrhea was at least manageable for me, aside from the embarrassment of sharing the bathroom with my newly assigned roommate. We turned out to be close in age but had almost nothing else in common. Each time I invited her to go somewhere with Grace, Emma, and me, she would go, but I could tell she never felt like she fit in. And honestly, we didn't feel like she did either. So now we had this slightly awkward relationship, sharing a tiny apartment with one bathroom, separated by a bathroom door made of glass, set on a barn-door-style metal rod up near the ceiling so that when you close it, about a one-inch gap remained between the left and right side of the door and the drywall. This allowed all the delightful smells and sounds to travel into the tiny basement's common living/kitchen area. Not the ideal situation for frequent explosive bowel movements.

As embarrassing and inconvenient Krka's Revenge was for me, I realized it was far worse for Grace. One day, as she was walking home from my apartment, the stomach bug attacked, and she had to step off the sidewalk into the bushes to go to the bathroom. Since Emma went back to Prague, Grace had the apartment all to herself, but this parasitic infection had impaired her to the point she couldn't eat anything and couldn't leave the house for fear of another urgent emergency situation.

Selfishly, I couldn't imagine having any fun in Croatia without Grace, so I visited a nearby pharmacy to find out if there was anything they could do to help. People were actually helpful in these foreign pharmacies, and I supposed that not constantly being worried about getting sued must have been the cause of the difference in approach toward customers. As I explained Grace's symptoms, the helpful folks behind the counter referred a few products and sent me on my way with some instructions.

After I dropped off her medicine, I googled a health food store to tackle my stomach problems next. My symptoms were milder and therefore merely inconvenient, but in anticipation of Grace getting better, I wanted to feel 100% so we could go have fun by the final week of our stay. This was the one time I thanked the heavens that I was staying near the city walls, close to all the touristy things. Inside the walls was a health food store offering a helpful array of teas and supplements. I found a liquid grapefruit seed extract that would have prevented our ails if we had known to put it in our water from the beginning.

Within a week, Grace was starting to feel better, though not fully recovered. She was going stir-crazy from being trapped in her apartment for so long, so we scheduled a spa day at a local hotel with a couple of other ladies from the digital nomad group. It was a welcome change to walk into a very modern and well-equipped Hilton situated right along the seaside. The spa promised beach access post-treatments, so we decided to hang out at the hotel pool first, then we would spend the rest of the day by the beach. Between having upset stomachs and the fact that the food at almost every place to eat inside the city walls pretty much sucked, we approached the hotel's food menu with gusto. Plus, all the servers were internationally trained, so English wasn't a problem there. Out of all the options we had, the thing we were craving the most was french fries, so we ordered an enormous plate and wolfed them down like we were planning to spend the day lounging in sweatpants, not sitting poolside in our bikinis.

After our treatments, we headed down a slightly deserted path to the spa beach access, where there was supposed to be music, lounge chairs, and a bar. While this is common for most travelers, it was a touch of luxury for us since we had been modest with our budgets and lived more like locals, out of rented apartments. Rather than finding a beach, it was more like a concrete slab, with a ladder leading down the side into the freezing Adriatic Sea. It felt like we weren't even there for minutes before Grace's stomach began to hurt, probably from the big batch of fries we ate a couple of hours ago. She headed back to the hotel in search of a restroom, and I went out to sit on a moss-covered rock, a little disappointed in our spa adventure.

Once I got uncomfortable on my hard stone seat, I stood up to find the moss had stained my turquoise bathing suit bottoms. There was a green mark on my ass that looked like a shit stain. Could this day get any less luxurious? I was over it and decided to head back up to the hotel to look for Grace. Wouldn't you know, the door we originally exited from in the spa was locked, so I had to walk all the way around the parking lot and enter the front of the hotel in my bathing suit. After eating a tub of fries. With a moss stain on my ass. Ugh. I was flush with embarrassment as I made my way through the large lobby and back into the spa locker rooms.

To my surprise, I found Grace in the locker room, fresh from a shower. "Why didn't you tell me you were leaving?" I asked. She sighed and began to tell me what just happened. If I thought I was embarrassed walking through the lobby, that was nothing. When Grace left my roommate and I at the seaside pool, she was in urgent need of a restroom. The french fries were wreaking havoc on her stomach, which apparently wasn't ready for all the starchy potatoes fried in hot oil and smattered with salt. She had scurried up the deserted path in search of a restroom, only to find the door we had exited out of the hotel spa locked. By this time, she was praying her bodily systems would hold off for a few moments, so she ran back to the path and stepped off into the trees and bushes just as her bowels let go. Squatting in the bushes, she was stuck for what felt like eternity. That is, until my newbie roommate walked by also headed toward the hotel restroom. Grace called out from behind the bush and asked to borrow her robe. Funny, but my roommate didn't even ask why; she simply handed it over without question. I can't imagine I would have done the same. I'd have asked all types of questions while she was still stuck in the bushes, like, "Why do you need my robe? What are you doing out there? I thought you were going to the bathroom?" She would have been forced to explain her situation out loud before I would have caught on.

Instead, Grace was able to make it to the spa door, mostly covered, but still with shit running down her legs. She had to act casual standing outside the door, waiting until my roommate could walk through the lobby, make her way back to the spa, and open the side door for her. Then, Grace beelined for the nearest shower to scrub herself and her swimsuit, free from her latest Krka's Revenge attack. She was putting on a new swimsuit, getting ready to head to the pool, which is when I walked in. I couldn't believe she thought ahead to bring a second swimsuit and that, after this experience, she was ready to head back out and try again.

Immediately, my annoyance over the tiny moss stain on my swimsuit disappeared. Not only was I hysterically laughing at Grace's rendition of the events, but if she could go through all that and still be in good spirits, then I needed to suck it up and quit moping because our beach/spa experience wasn't exactly what I expected. We decided that since the main hotel is situated close to a bathroom, we would hang out there a little bit longer. It was somewhat relaxing to have no more expectations for this day, and even though it wasn't the nicest spa in the world, the time lying by the pool was much needed to reset the brain. We Ubered back to our apartments with a lifted mood and one more interesting story to tell.

Grace and I were bored of Split, though I could say it was probably the perfect place for us to have stomach issues. The food inside the city walls was complete garbage, designed for tourists there for a short stay who were willing to stuff themselves full of bad pizza and pastries. We inquired about where the locals eat, hoping to find some local gems, but were told that the locals eat at home due to the country's economic conditions. Great. So we were stuck eating shit food unless we cooked at home, which for me means even shittier food since I can't cook.

Before this trip, I wouldn't have been able to imagine getting restless living in a location for only one month. How could one month possibly be enough? But I was restless and ready to leave this place. We decided to make our final week more interesting by moving around a bit and booked a last-minute Airbnb in Hvar for a few days, followed by a couple of days in Dubrovnik. Our house in Hvar was the complete opposite of my basement apartment outside the walls of Split. It was open and spacious, with windows overlooking the ocean and the sun shining brightly throughout the entire home. I felt better already!

We were within walking distance to the main shops in town, and our path there was along the water, so every moment of every activity felt like a vacation. I mean, the water was still too fucking cold to go jump in or sunbathe properly, but seeing the ocean everywhere I looked felt soothing. In town, there were stone paths and stairways between the shops and restaurants that were more visually appealing than the stone walls in Split. For some reason, the stone in Split felt like a prison, whereas Hvar felt more like a vacation spot in Italy. At night, we went to the local clubs, which were surprisingly packed. Plenty of flirtatious guys half our age made us start questioning their probable mommy issues. Last month, I was shocked by this in Prague when it happened the first time, but now it was kind of a thing. We would go out to the clubs, man-boys come up and flirt, we would ask how old they are, and I would tell them I have a child their age. They would either retreat in horror or try harder. Rinse. Repeat.

Grace had become a good friend through all of it. We navigated all these new cities with an ease, which would typically be challenging in a new friendship. If we entered a club and thought it was lame, we would make eye contact, give a nod of the head and it's off to the next one. When she was having boyfriend trouble with her man back home, I gave her the honest truths she didn't want to hear. When I slipped and fell on the stairs outside our Hvar house, she laughed hysterically and reached for her camera to get a picture before even thinking to help me up. While these may not be your typical dictionary definitions of friendship, for me, they are authentic bonds that you share only with someone you are willing to be yourself around. It made me want the trip to last longer since Croatia was the last scheduled stop on our itinerary.

Fortunately, Emma kept in touch during her unexpected month in Prague. She shared with us that she was planning a stop in Dublin on her way back home. When I checked on plane tickets, I found it would be much cheaper to fly back to the States from Dublin, so I tacked that onto the end of the trip. Desperate to delay our return home, even if only a little, the three of us agreed that since we were departing Croatia as Oktoberfest was beginning, we should stop off in Germany for a few days. The cost was so minuscule, how could we not? When else would I have the chance to hit up Oktoberfest for only a few hundred dollars? It was an opportunity I couldn't pass up. I'd never been to Germany, and I am part German after all. The deal was sealed, tickets were booked, and Oktoberfest was official. Grace had to get home following that, so Emma and I would continue to Dublin on our own. After that, I'd return home in plenty of time to spend the holidays with Sage and my family.

Oktoberfoot

Emma rejoined us, and it felt like coming home for the holidays after your first semester at university. Everything felt right as we made our way through the Croatia airport to catch our Munich flight. When we arrived at the gate, we looked around in fear that they changed our departure at the last minute. There was no one sitting and waiting to board. An agent let us know the last bus to the plane was waiting for us. They must board early in Croatia! The gate was nothing more than sliding glass doors that exited the airport to an awaiting bus, which carted all the passengers out to the tarmac, where we boarded the portable metal stairs that had been wheeled out alongside the plane.

The three of us scurried toward the open bus doors while everyone inside scowled at us for holding up the driver. Emma squeezed into the crowd and turned around just in time to see me step off the curb, roll my ankle, and come careening through the open doors face first with my arms flailing. One arm caught underneath my body and saved my face from smacking into the floor of the bus. Since my phone was in my hand, it made a loud *thwack* as it hit the floor and anyone who wasn't staring before now turned their head to see me sprawled out on the bus floor.

I gasped for breath, and the moment air re-entered my lungs, I spit out hysterical laughter, thinking about Emma watching this all happen in slow motion. Grace stepped in behind me, already wiping her eyes from laughing so hard. Everyone on the bus collectively let out a sigh, seeing that I wasn't spewing blood or brains all over the place and wouldn't be further delaying their travel plans. My ability to laugh at myself somewhat surprised me. At home I'd always been so concerned about what other people thought; was I put together enough, did I present myself properly? Imaginably, the past four months of living out of one suitcase and no blow dryer might have inched me one step closer to accepting myself.

It seemed like we were in Germany before I knew it, and I was in awe of how organized the city streets were. The public transportation was easy to use, bike lanes were well-marked, and nobody even so much as jaywalked. It was as though I was an alien that had finally identified my mother ship. We didn't have much time scheduled there, so we sped through our normal routines of acclimating. Instead of doing full walking tours, we pulled up Google Maps and decided to walk around Justizpalast (Palace of Justice) admiring The Karlstor, a city gate built in the 14th century. We ate amazing sausages and, of course, drank our fair share of beer, challenging each other to see who could hold their stein the longest (they are five pounds, so I reckoned that could be considered my workout). Beer halls were everywhere, but we found some of the most famous that had been recommended were offputting. They seemed to be tourist traps, adorned with cheap furniture similar to what I've seen at a Taco Bell back home, but styled to appear as though it was traditional Bavarian.

We were filled with anticipation the next day as we headed off to our first Oktoberfest. While tradition holds that you wear authentic outfits, called Trachten (women wear dirndl dresses and men wear the infamous leather lederhosen shorts), we hadn't planned and packed for this, nor did we find it necessary to fork out the money to rent these costumes. Instead, when Emma went back to Prague to visit her new beau, she stopped by our favorite bar and picked up matching shirts for us. We headed off to the festival in matching Beer Geek shirts, anticipating a day full of excellent local beer and eats.

The subway was packed full of people in Trachten and energies were running high as we spilled out into the streets outside the festival grounds. Ah, the infamous Oktoberfest! We entered and walked around, initially confused by where the festivities were taking place. The costumes would suggest we were in the right place, but this venue was quite like a giant parking lot with tents, cheap vendor kiosks, and carnival rides. Was this it? Without the lederhosen, I could have mistaken myself for being at the Arizona State Fair. We decided the oooh and ahhh must be inside the tents, which were rumored to be spectacular. As we wandered inside a few of the beer tents, they were indeed designed to look like the famous beer halls. Tent ceilings were decorated to look like the skies of olden times, with the outlines of less modern buildings around the edges, paintings of men in their lederhosen or riding horseback attempting to give it an old-world feel.

But like the tourist spots we had already been to, they were packed full of people standing body to body, with long lines and nowhere to sit. We walked through, looked up at the ceilings and the decor, and then on to the next (if we could even get in). Finally, we found one with a spot to sit outside the tent at some picnic tables. Glad to finally rest our feet, we ordered steins and pretzels and prepared to enjoy our authentic Oktoberfest experience. We lifted the heavy steins and cheers to our adventure, proceeding to drink an obscene amount of what tastes like Germany's version of Bud Light.

While it wasn't the experience we had anticipated, we were happy to be off our feet for a moment and elected to people-watch the craziness around us. As we looked out into the crowds, a young guy walked up to our table and sat down. He said he lost his friends and his phone and proceeded to lay his head on our table and pass out. We were able to rouse him enough to find out what hotel he was in and asked him what the hell he was on. Apparently, he had done a shitload of Bavarian cocaine and was out of his mind. We offered to call him an Uber, and he freely handed over his wallet with no questions asked. The kid was only 21 years old and was ripe for someone to steal all that he had left. Grace handed him the wallet and lectured him about putting it away. She orders him not to give it to anyone while ordering an Uber to his hotel. We send him on his merry way and hoped he arrived at his hotel and at least remembered his room number. Either way, he was probably better off in the hotel lobby than passed out around here.

Not that he would be alone. People were passed out *everywhere*. Laying on the ground or benches. As we walked by one of the city's many decorative potted planters on the street corner, the bright and colorful flowers were being squashed by a man with a skull tattoo on his forearm. He appeared to have toppled over backward into the plant; his arms reached wide open towards the heavens, his button-fly jeans only unevenly half-buttoned. We couldn't help but start snapping pictures of all the awkward bodies splayed out in public places. It was definitely something to see, but not something I wanted to do for a second day. Emma and Grace agreed; we'd seen enough. We backtracked toward the train it felt like we just got off of, to go back into town for some quality eats and craft beer.

On our final day, we boarded the train one last time to the airport. Emma and I were flying off to Dublin, and Grace was staying in an airport hotel for one more night before her early morning flight back to Texas. We were somber and a bit cranky, so we sat quietly for most of the train ride, each of us in our own heads. The thought loop I was stuck in revolved around saying goodbye to Grace. Though I had known this moment would come, I was not quite prepared for it. None of us had any huge emotional acknowledgment, though; isn't that funny?

My crusty exterior always protected me from showing emotion. No one expected me to cry at funerals or jump up and down with excitement when they shared happy news. Grace had seen through my protective facade, though, and I wasn't sure how to simply express to my new friend that I would miss her. Before I could dwell on it any further, Grace broke the silence, "You guys, I think we are going the wrong way. I don't think this train is going to the airport." Emma and I snapped our heads to attention. We didn't have much of a buffer on time, so if this train was headed in the wrong direction, we would miss our flight. As we started to listen intently to the stops being announced in German, we consulted the map of the train route posted on the wall inside the car. Sure enough, the next stop was announced, and it was several stops away from where we boarded, but in the direction *away* from the airport, not towards it. Somehow, we had boarded the wrong train. Unsure how it happened, but certain we needed to get off before we went any further the wrong way, we grabbed our luggage and pushed our way toward the doors at the upcoming stop.

    We exited the platform and rushed to the other side so we could board the next train heading in the correct direction. Tensions were even higher now that our flights were at stake, and we were on edge waiting for the next train to arrive. After a short wait that felt like an eternity, we finally started off in the correct direction. Once aboard, we began to bid our choppy farewells to Grace while the train was still moving. No one was worried about the right thing to say at that point, so it did take some of the pressure off. Emma and I were off and running as soon as the doors opened at the airport stop. Literally running.

Since my episode falling into the bus at the airport in Croatia, I was trying to be extra careful as we pushed our luggage through the airport, running at full speed. Fun fact about the airport in Munich, we had quite a ways to go before getting to baggage check. Most of the airports I'd been in had the ticketing and baggage area almost immediately upon entering the airport. We weren't so lucky this time. By the time the ticketing counter was in sight, we were out of breath and sweating like Olympic track stars. After checking our luggage, we ran to security and then to the gate, half expecting to be told we were out of luck. To our surprise, our plane hadn't left yet. We boarded, and by the time we landed over two hours later, our pulse was finally back down to a resting rate.

In Dublin, we caught a car from the airport and quickly agreed the rumors about Irish people seemed to be true in our case study of one. They actually are the friendliest people on earth. Our driver told us stories of Ireland's history the entire way, clearly proud of his country and heritage. Emma was staying at an Airbnb with some lovely hosts, and I was staying in a hotel in the heart of town. The vibe was definitely different than I'd come to expect the last couple of months, always having either Emma or Grace around 24/7. We had to make short work of seeing the sights in the few days we had. We threw ourselves into local pubs and restaurants, booked a tour of the Guinness factory and a local castle, and ogled the amazing architecture in the city. Locals could tell I was American by my accent, and many of them extended their condolences on the tragedy that had recently taken place. We learned that a shooter had opened fire on a concert in Las Vegas from a surrounding hotel window. Numerous concertgoers were wounded, many were dead, and I am sure all were emotionally scarred. Dare I say, the Irish locals were more bereft about the event than I was, as an American. That sealed it; the rumors were absolutely true; these were the nicest people on the planet.

After learning to pour a Guinness the proper way and reminding myself how much whiskey reminded me of bad high school parties while on a tour of the Jameson facility, I was back at the airport in a blip. Emma and I said our goodbyes without much fanfare the day before, and I sat on the tarmac while my flight got delayed. After a quick jaunt over to Amsterdam, I'd change planes, and then it was on to the U.S. Once we landed in Amsterdam, I was thrust into flashbacks of our run through the airport in Munich. The delay in Dublin had caused me to land as my next flight was already boarding. Our flight attendant directed us to the gate of our already boarding flight and assured us our luggage would be transferred in time. As soon as my feet hit the terminal,

I was running again. Full speed with my backpack on my back. This airport felt bigger than Munich, and my chubby thighs were burning. Navigating the signs to the correct gate was more challenging when running full out. Struggling to breathe, I arrived at the gate two minutes after they had closed the doors. I was advised that I wasn't allowed to board, which might have sent me into an angry spiral, except the airline agents were so incredibly helpful and nice. The agent placed me on another flight a few hours later while I made a mental note to come back and spend some time in Amsterdam.

Defeated, I headed to find something to eat so I could sit down and catch my breath. I needed to text Sage and let her know I wouldn't be on the original flight since she was planning to pick me up from the airport. Luckily, the delay only set me back a few hours, so I wouldn't be stuck there all night. Not that Amsterdam would be a horrible place to be stuck in. But I'd said my goodbyes to Emma and Grace and come to terms with this portion of my journey ending. I was ready to move on to the next chapter. Funny, I've always been that way. As painful as endings can be, the idea of the next chapter has always excited me. There will be a new story to tell, and when something is over, it's over.

Thinking back to last spring when this travel idea had originally hatched, I evaluated the trip compared to my expectations. It turned out nothing like I expected, though it was hard to even conjure up what that was in my mind any longer. The only point of reference I had before getting on that first flight was from the movie *Eat. Pray. Love.* Julia Robert's amazing apartment in Italy and making a dear friend over a cappuccino order doesn't exactly align with my dirty apartment in Spain or becoming friends with Emma & Grace on the train to sample wine in the Douro Valley, but they are my version of the "Eat" portion of the story. Except I think in my version, it would need to be labeled, *Drink*. A few of my favorite memories of the past summer floated through my mind and I could only hope to hang on to them, but I was ready to go home for the holidays and spend time with Sage. The idea of not being with her over the holidays would be unbearable. Rather than try and extend this trip any longer, I was suddenly bursting to get home and experience home life from this new travel perspective I'd gained. Back in May, the woman who had stepped on the plane seemed so long ago and almost foreign to me now; could I step back into her life? Did I even have a life?

Soul-crushing routine.

That's how I would have described my life prior to travel. Each day was like the last, with nothing notably different on the horizon. But now I had lived out of one suitcase, lived in other people's homes, and worked without ever going to an office. This nomadism started to heal me, even though I wasn't ready to do the deep work yet.

What does any of that have to do with healing? Healing requires you to be present in the moment. Which

I would argue that most of us aren't focused on being present when our lives are on autopilot. Get up. Drive to work. Wait, first stop at Starbz. Do nearly the same thing every day for corporate-y McCorporate. Drive home. Eat dinner. Have a drink to unwind. Rinse and repeat. How many times have you blinked, and several weeks, months, or even years have passed with nothing much happening? Looking back, everything is a blur of sameness, and you wonder when life passed you by.

Now, contrast that with arriving in a new country on a Saturday morning. You check into the Airbnb you will stay in for the next month. This isn't a vacation; you are here to live like a local. After stopping at an ATM for local currency and needing to use a currency conversion app to ensure you are taking out $200 instead of $2,000, you set off to buy groceries. At the store, you realize you need Google Translate to make sure you are actually buying salt, not sugar. Then, at the cash register, you start to count out the fresh bills from the ATM and realize how much you rely on the familiarity of your local currency to distinguish a dollar from a quarter. Now, you have to read the face of each bill and coin, doing the math in your head. It's basic math, but it's something you haven't done since, well, maybe elementary school. You've been in a new locale for all of two hours and you've used parts of your brain that are in permanent hibernation at home. Needless to say, you'll learn the currency and route to your Airbnb soon enough, but the tiny challenges will continue to pepper your everyday actions. New connections are forming in the brain, like growing new muscle. These ordinary actions that you take for granted at home become new adventures and experiences.

This was a recipe for me becoming more aware and present in life. There was no possible way I could have formed all these new neural connections in my brain and return home to put everything on autopilot again. I couldn't wait to get home and experience my hometown through a new lens.

CHAPTER 3

Home for the Holidays

Sage was behind the wheel of my 4Runner outside Phoenix Sky Harbor; it was already October, but I started sweating within a few moments of standing on the airport arrivals curb. My luggage had been lost on the last leg of the flight, so I grabbed my backpack and hopped in the passenger seat. We greeted with an undramatic 'hello,' like I'd been gone on a short weekend trip. Given our lack of emotional theatrics, an onlooker might not have guessed how close a relationship we shared. She looked exactly the same as when I left in May. What was I expecting? She had turned 21 while I was gone. Did I expect that to cause her to grow two inches taller or change her blonde hair to auburn? But she was the same daughter I had left in May, and the world had continued to turn without me. In the last several months, I'd accomplished so many things I would have previously thought impossible. I made friends. I took trains, taxis, and planes by myself. I had a new sense of confidence emerging so I felt like this was somehow visible on my exterior body, but if anyone noticed it, nobody acknowledged it. This was the same old chubby version of myself but without the coordinated clothing and shiny straight hair.

Of course, all the gifts and souvenirs I bought for everyone along the way were in my suitcase, so I told Sage I would have to get those to her when my luggage was returned. Not that she wanted anything; she was always independent and never asked for anything. She made the short drive to her apartment so I could take my car from there. Excitedly, I remembered that I had bought a gift for her and her boyfriend while I was at the Amsterdam airport. Those items were in my backpack and not floating around the U.S. in my lost luggage. "Wait, before you go, I brought you guys something from Amsterdam, and it's in my carry-on." I lifted the hatch on my 4Runner and turned to hand the souvenir bag to Sage, but she wasn't there. I called her name again, and she continued to stand near the driver's side door. "Come here," I told her, "I have something for you." To my surprise, she said, "Mom, I'm not standing on the sidewalk outside my apartment while you try to give me drugs!"

"Drugs?! What the fuck are you talking about?"

"I know you brought me marijuana from Amsterdam, and I'm not taking it."

"You think I smuggled weed from Amsterdam into the U.S.? And that after committing a felony to do so, I would give that weed to *you*? Are you insane?" By this point, I was cracking up, thinking that this whole interaction was hysterical.

After ensuring her that I, in fact, did not have any drugs in my possession and was trying to give her something completely legal, she finally came around the back of the car. She rolled her eyes once she saw the matching pot leaf socks I had bought for her and her boyfriend. This pot was perfectly legal to carry on the plane. "Thanks," she said sarcastically.

Ah, it was good to be home!

Coming home initially was kind of a whirlwind, with my birthday falling a week after I got home, then Thanksgiving, then Christmas. I made plans with all my family and friends while telling the same story of my adventures over and over again. It brought me so much joy to re-live all those moments and gave me some time to reflect. Everyone wanted to know where I was going next, as I was scheduled to leave again in January. While I had some ideas, I hadn't fully decided where I was going yet. Except for one friend, who flat-out asked, "What are you running from?" In my mind, I wasn't running at all. But was I? Was this all a distraction from having to process my life? Was I actually running away from my thoughts, my feelings, my fears, and all the work I needed to do to move forward with my life? Undoubtedly, yes, but I wasn't ready to dig into those feelings yet. I had another trip to plan.

Originally, I had planned to pick back up with the same group of digital nomads when they hit South America in February, but I no longer felt I needed someone else planning all my travel, choosing a roommate for me, and determining my destinations. Something told me it was time for me to go solo, make my own travel arrangements, and be free to go wherever I wanted, whenever I wanted. With one exception. Grace and I had been keeping up on WhatsApp, and when I finally decided on my next location, Peru, she agreed to meet me there for a couple of weeks. This gave me one more thing to look forward to, and between that and visiting with everyone locally, I knew the holidays would fly by.

♥

Ugh, Doctors

During the months spent in Europe, my clothes had progressively become tighter and tighter. I'd always had thick assets; even when I was a size zero, this girl still had booty. Before travel, I'd already gained plenty of extra padding, but not at the alarming rate of ten pounds in five months. If I didn't get this shit under control, I'd have to buy a whole new wardrobe. My addiction to travel added so many places to the 'want to see' list that I couldn't fathom taking money away from the travel bucket to buy new clothes. Besides, at the rate I was gaining, I feared all that would be left to buy were leggings and moo moos. Although that did sound pretty comfortable.

When I initially started gaining, I suspected it was due to age and hormones. Let's get something straight:

women are blessed with the ability to have children and, as a reward, 'get' to experience menopause, a delightful combination of forgetfulness, night sweats, and getting fat. WTF - thanks for that! It's been a real pleasure. Please find new ways to destroy my body. Maybe at age forty, all women should receive a Girl Scout sash, but instead of "campfire" badges, we earn a patch for every pound we gain or new symptoms we acquire. If that were the case, I would have achieved a new badge of honor when my bloodwork revealed hypothyroidism. Symptoms include…..more weight gain! Yay, just what I needed. I might need two sashes.

Since traveling internationally required keeping prescription medications in their original packaging in case customs questioned you, I had decided not to bring any prescriptions, including hypothyroid medication, with me when I left for Europe. It didn't seem to be helping, and surely it didn't make me lose any weight or get my formerly clear-thinking brain back. However, now that I hadn't taken it in five months and was tipping the scales at a record-high weight, I thought perhaps the medication *had* been doing something after all.

To top it off, my opinion of the medical system in the United States has been diminishing over the years. Slowly, I started moving over to naturopathic doctors and seeking alternative ways to approach 'treatment.' Giving up all my prescription medications felt pretty good, so I was a bit reluctant to make the appointment with my doctor to have my thyroid rechecked. Vanity won in the end because I didn't want to continue to see this larger version of myself in the mirror every day.

Fully expecting to refill my thyroid meds after my bloodwork came back, I was surprised when the doctor called and said my thyroid came back normal. *Normal?* Funny, I quit the medicine, and the problem fixed itself. Wasn't nature grand! That encouraged me to continue my quest for more natural solutions and perhaps to believe that the body truly is miraculous and heals itself.

On the flip-side, it meant I had nothing and no one to blame for my giant ass and thunder thighs. It was only *my* actions causing me to pack on the pounds. As I reflected on the massive amount of cheap lager I had consumed in Prague, the gin & tonics of Valencia, all the wine tours, Oktoberfest, steins in Germany, and Guinness in Dublin, it was almost embarrassing to think I was trying to blame this all on my thyroid. "Jesus, woman, close your damn mouth," my body was screaming. If my liver could talk it was probably using much stronger language than that. Before my travel, I had known I needed to cut the drinking down because I was using it to cope, and it was sad to be at home drinking a bottle of wine every night *alone*. But when you're out in new places, sampling the local crafts and hanging out with friends, it didn't seem so bad. In all honesty, I probably drank more in Europe than before I left home, but it didn't feel as *wrong*, so I didn't pay attention. Now that I was home, I'd use the next couple of months to get my shit together, or so I told myself.

My doctor interrupted the false promises I was making myself; apparently, he wasn't done yet. Although my thyroid had come back normal, my CBC (complete blood count) was not. This wasn't a new story; my blood had been wonky for a long time. At least since ten years ago, when my naturopathic doctor had identified my high platelet count and insisted I immediately stop taking the birth control I'd been consuming since my late teens. Evidently, a side effect of birth control was blood clots - who knew? Maybe the countless number of ObGyns who prescribe it each year. But does our healthcare system require a CBC prior to prescribing it to ensure you aren't at risk? Fuck no. Just scribble it down on a scrap of paper and dutifully deliver it to your local pharmacy. Why do we so blindly hand our health care decisions over to companies who primarily care about profits over people?

Over the years in between, I had seen doctors off and on to monitor the situation. The term cancer had been thrown around lightly, but what they were really concerned about was the nasty one, Leukemia. For a while I saw my hematologist daily, then weekly, then monthly, but it was always the same experience. They would try and work it into a big deal, probably no fault of theirs, with all the ridiculous malpractice claims in the U.S. Every time they tested, I was always clear of Leukemia, so I no longer worried about my consistently abnormal blood. They could never pinpoint any specific solution and, at best, wanted me to keep coming back in for endless testing. Finally, growing tired of the experience and never experiencing any relief from my minor symptoms, I decided I didn't need medical intervention. I was so over it. All the testing and scare tactics, time and money, for no more answers and me having to find my own solutions anyway. After spending too much time researching the various types of cancer they thought it could be, everything I learned was fairly comforting. Yes, I said 'cancer' and 'comforting' in the same sentence. This was nothing more than a disorder that you could live with your whole life, and aside from a few potential issues, it wasn't very life-altering. And so, I didn't concern myself with it.

So here I was, trying to explain to my general practitioner why I didn't want to follow up with another specialist after all these years. He was a pretty laid-back guy, so when he insisted that I should see someone, I felt inclined to do so. Even though I liked to act tough, I was as influenceable as the rest of the population, I guess. He agreed to refer me to someone good if I would promise to make an appointment before I left the country again. There were only a couple of months I would be home during the holidays, so his office assisted with the initial scheduling to ensure the typical new patient delay was avoided. God, I had even more disdain for our whole healthcare system after traveling in Europe.

Admittedly, I did like the new hematologist much better than my last. He was very thorough in his questioning, and he had gone through my previous records and found several tests he felt should have been run but hadn't. Here we go again, with them wanting to poke and prod some more. I was more than skeptical and impatient with the idea, and he knew it. He looked at me in what I perceived to be a condescending way and asked if I knew the definition of cancer. Yep, doc, I got it… uncontrolled division of abnormal cells. I presumed this was his way of telling me I should take it more seriously. Except that, I've never much liked authority figures, so trying to mansplain only made me more defiant. I shrugged my shoulders with feigned nonchalance and said, "I know." Knowing me, I probably lifted my chin in defiance at the same time, but I can't confirm that actually happened. Besides, I already knew it was unlikely my issues would lead to any type of treatment, so I felt like trying to use the word cancer to scare people into submission was a cheap trick.

All the fucking tests he wanted to run were ridiculous. My body had been drained of blood from all the vials and I was pretty sure I looked like Bella in Twilight after she became a vampire with iridescently pale skin. Of course, they made that look pretty in the movie, but in real life, I was the same slightly overweight blonde with half as much blood and slightly bruised veins. Since they've drained all my life force, he moved on to recommending the test I'd declined so many times in the past: a bone marrow biopsy.

First of all, I hadn't told many, if anyone, about the nature of my blood *disorder*. My terminology was specific on purpose: I truly believe that disease is nothing but disordered cells and energy in the body, so I feel disorder is a more appropriate term. So, back to why I haven't done the biopsy. Well, it was twofold; first, it fucking hurts, and second, I was supposed to bring someone with me. The last time my doctor recommended it, he described it as a manual procedure that required a large needle to be jabbed into my femur bone so they could pull marrow out. He made no bones (pun intended) about the fact that it would be incredibly painful. In fact, he recommended that I bring someone with me to hold my hand through the process or comfort me if I cried. *Fuck that.* I was not holding hands and crying in some frigid office while laying on butcher paper that looks like it should be lining an elementary school hallway with murals painted on it. That was a no for me, thanks.

The new doctor assured me that these biopsies had progressed exponentially in the last few years, and they were now performed in a hospital with high-tech equipment that rendered them relatively pain-free. He could call the hospital and make an appointment for me since he was concerned about me being able to complete this task before I left the country. Actually, concerned isn't a severe enough word. I think his exact words were, "I strongly recommend you cancel your travel plans. Depending on the results of this biopsy, you may need immediate care that you can't receive in South America." To which my answer was (of course), "I'm not canceling. I'll be in South America for at least four months, so any recommended procedures will have to wait."

My attitude was getting bolder and more defiant, but I still agreed to allow him to make the appointment. Since he finally gained my compliance on the issue, he went on to explain the three possible outcomes after the biopsy. If I received one of the three results, he explained, it would require a bone marrow transplant. Ew. The thought of them sucking my bone marrow out and *putting someone else's shit in my body* creeped me out. I wouldn't even walk barefoot in a hotel room because I don't want the bottom of my feet touching other people's dead skin cells and stray hairs. But this guy is talking about squirting some rando's bone juice in me?

Doc was looking at me funny, and I realized it was because I said, "Ew" out loud. Perhaps he never had a patient respond in this manner. Do normal people get sucked into the fear-mongering? It wasn't to say I was resilient to fear, but my concern was more around the yet more invasive treatment of a worst-case scenario. "No thanks, Doc," I told him, feeling like I needed to offer an explanation for my reaction, "That is gross." Besides, I was pretty sure there was nothing wrong with my bone marrow anyway. I'm not educated with years of medical school, but it was *my* body and that was my gut feeling. Still, I scheduled the biopsy for a week before my departure, which gave good ol' Doc even more angina. This was almost becoming a fun game for me. It was like he had never traveled before. "How will

I reach you with your results?" he asked. Um, the way you reach everyone else...I'm not taking a rocket ship into space; my flight is to Peru, not Mars. Call me, e-mail me, send a fucking carrier pigeon, I don't care.

Pretty impressively, I only tried to cancel the procedure once. Even though I didn't want to deal with this while also trying to wrap up at work and home to travel again, there was a nagging little voice of fear that told me to do it. Damn these doctors for getting into my head. On the scheduled day, I Ubered to the hospital for the new and improved, high-tech aspiration of my bone marrow. Of course, they fucking lied by saying this new procedure was painless and they would put me under. Well, by 'under,' they meant they would jab me with whatever toxic cocktail was in the syringe, and then I *might go under* or... I might stay awake. Um, okay, that wasn't what I was originally told, but whatever, as long as it doesn't hurt. Yes, I am a giant pussy and only care about whether it is going to hurt. Then I felt the needle shoot into my pelvic bone, right above my ass crack. It *was* quick but not painless. That needle had to be gigantic because I swear I felt it penetrate the bone. Plus, the hole it left behind was visible to the naked eye. They popped a bandaid on it to keep the area clean, and I still had a bandaid on it when I boarded my plane for Peru.

CHAPTER 4

Here I Go Again

Getting back on a plane felt more like home to me than actually being at home. Rather than being a mundane routine, it was still exciting, like visiting a familiar lover. While you have no idea exactly what will happen, you know you will enjoy it. There is the initial flush of dopamine and serotonin that makes anything seem dealwithable. It consumed all my thoughts, money, and free time. Except, unlike a lover, there will be no negative reflections after an ugly breakup. No double life to accidentally discover. Travel swallowed up this void I used to fill with relationships. I wasn't lonely, nor did I desire a relationship, as I had new countries to provide me with all the excitement I could handle. This time, my suitor would be the country of Peru. My flight to Lima started in Arizona, with a stop in Texas and then on to Peru. I boarded alone and met up with Grace once I landed in Texas. We hadn't seen each other since I flew from Germany to Ireland, so we spent the entire flight to Lima catching up on all that had happened over the holidays at home.

Even if there hadn't been three months that we hadn't seen each other, I still don't think we would have run out of things to talk about. Grace was one of those rare people who would let me go deep into the details, analyzing everything and leaving nothing out. We could talk for hours without running out of topics. Even though we sometimes dove into some deep shit, the conversations often involved a lot of laughing and positive energy.

Grace decided to join me for my first few weeks in Peru because she had some free time available before some work travel required her to attend conferences. Have I mentioned she is way more outgoing than me? She would easily jump on a Facebook Live and talk to a bunch of people without batting an eye. That was a stark contrast to my ability to freeze and forget how to even say my name if a camera was on. Actually, back in Europe, she was the one who taught me how to take a selfie. I never wanted pictures of myself before, so I never learned the skill. Not that I was much better now, but at least I had a few more memories stored in my iPhone than if she hadn't taught me.

In Europe, we had the safety net of our digital nomad group making all our reservations and flights and assigning a local guide to answer our questions in each location. I had no regrets about traveling that way to start, but I also felt like I was working up to something bigger, like traveling by myself. To ease myself into South America, I booked the first 30 days with a different type of travel group and left the rest of my agenda open. Perhaps someone in the group would enlighten me on places I should go and see. In general, I thought I'd probably head further south - Chile, Argentina, and probably not Brazil due to the paperwork needed ahead of time. As an uber-rigid, organized girl, the open-ended blank slate of this trip was surprisingly refreshing. Perhaps I should have been more nervous than I was, but it was like I was proving to myself that a list of descriptive adjectives doesn't define who I have to be. I could enjoy planning and also completely fly by the seat of my pants. Whoever I wanted to be was entirely up to me.

♥

Peru

The first week passed like part II of your favorite movie, with Grace and I putzing around town, getting the lay of the land, and sampling all the craft beer bars. But by week two, changes began to occur. Even though it was only three months after Europe, things have changed. Both Grace and I were in different places in our life. We had burdens to bear that felt too heavy to even discuss with each other. Grace's north star happens to be yoga and meditation. In Europe, she joined yoga studios in various locations, but I never once was inclined to go with her.

In Peru, things were different. I was still waiting on the results from my biopsy, and thoughts about my health wormed their way into the caverns of my subconscious. No more gluttonous behavior. Okay...maybe a little less gluttonous behavior. In true Grace fashion, she found not only a yoga studio but an organic, vegan cafe that prepared juice cleanses. Somehow, I found myself agreeing to a 3-day juice cleanse. There was no part of this I was prepared for. I'd never juiced before, but I assumed the evacuation of my bowels was normal, or at least the desired effect of eliminating toxins from my body. For three days I started each morning by walking to the café and picking up 12 glass bottles filled with brightly colored vegetables: 6 for me and 6 for Grace. The next day, I'd bring back the empties and retrieve another rainbow of veggies, reduced to brightly colored pulp.

In 40-something years, I'd never truly appreciated the texture and consistency of food. The process of chewing is, quite honestly, not something I had ever given much thought to. Suddenly, without the need to chew, I violently missed it. Drinking my nutrition left me feeling unsatiated, and the full-octane nutrition of this cleanse was completely foreign to my body. After two days, I couldn't take it any longer, and I gave in to my cravings. I was on a risotto kick pre-juice cleanse, so I found a restaurant not far from my apartment and dove into a bowl. If I could have literally dove into it, I would have slathered it all over me. It wasn't only the sensation of the creamy taste that hit the taste buds that was so pleasing. It was the fact that my jaw finally had something to do....chew. After chewing and savoring a few bites, I realized something. The risotto wasn't even that good. I'd been obsessing so much over my lack of solid food that a dirty sock would seemingly taste good between my teeth right now. As I became present again, it was clear that my issue was a mental mind fuck, not an actual need for solid food. Since I'd broken the cleanse, I decided to stop the juicing, but I'd follow protocol from here out on how to introduce solid, raw food back into my diet. Grace finished her cleanse, and we stocked up on organic nuts, some raw bars; and we decided to try dining on sushi and avoid red meat completely.

At the same time, we started taking yoga at a studio a few blocks away. There was a period of time, many years ago when I took Bikram yoga. Bikram is the exact same flow of movements during a 90-minute class, which works for me because my memory sucks. Also, I like my workouts a little out of the ordinary, and Bikram is performed in a heated room, so you sweat your balls off the whole time (I'm just guessing if I had balls, I would have sweated them off...). My point is I'd never taken 'regular' yoga, so my knowledge of flow yoga shit was pretty nonexistent. This would be my first flow yoga class, and to top it off, the instruction would be entirely in Spanish. Between my lack of knowledge of yoga poses and my lack of understanding of Spanish, I could only pick up the cue for downward dog. I listened intently for the word "Perro" and pop my butt into the air while straining my neck and looking at the rest of the participants upside-down, trying to follow their lead on what to do next. Grace was trying to cue me from her mat on my left-hand side, so between all of that, I was pretty pleased with completing my first class and kinda-sorta being able to do all the things.

Before we took more classes, Grace taught me the standard Vinyasa. My skill wasn't anywhere near expert level, but it would get me through a few of the repetitive movements in class without having to crane my neck to see others in the room. We went to class a few more times during Grace's two-week visit, and I liked it well enough. It wasn't CrossFit, but it felt healthy in a relaxing kind of way. Since I had shown an interest in this lifestyle, Grace hesitantly introduced me to meditation. She started me off with some meditations on Spotify that I dubbed 'woo woo lite' style meditation. Each night before bed, I put my headphones on and let the healing affirmations wash over me. In two weeks' time, I'd tried juicing, yoga and meditation. This hippie shit was unexpected but was unquestionably filling a major gap in my being; spirituality.

Growing up, we were raised Christian. Our mother took us to church every Sunday and Wednesday. She was active in the church and tried diligently to instill these values in us. Probably innately, my brother and I had good moral compasses but were not inclined to believe in religion. My brother is a scientist, so he probably had more reasons than I did. For me, it was more about not liking people telling me what to do or believe. Anything organized seemed untrustworthy to me...religion, government, big medicine, social media. My earliest memory of thinking Christianity was fucked up related to missionaries. I learned that Christian missionaries went to other countries to convert the people there to Christianity so that they could "be saved." Always an anxious child, I think I nearly had a panic attack, asking, "What about the children in China that weren't born into Christianity? If a missionary doesn't find them, then they go to hell? That's not fair!" Why my elementary school brain assumed the non-Christians were located in China, I have no idea. But for me, that concept stayed with me throughout the years, and I had a general mistrust of all religions because I knew that much of what I was hearing wasn't true. One religion can't be right, while the rest are wrong. Who decides? Besides, all religion is based on human interpretation of shit they don't understand. Why can't we, as humans, admit we don't understand where the fuck we came from or why, and leave it at that?

Unfortunately for me, there was a component of life that involves some level of spirituality, for whatever reason. Since I rejected religion at such a young age, I never looked into alternative outlets for this human need for spirituality. It was certainly an area I felt disconnected in, although I would have never been able to define it until now. Meditation, breathing, energy flow, the universe...these were all concepts I felt more comfortable allowing in my life than I did with any organized religious concepts. Even though as I learned more, I identified the similarity of my comfort in leaving things to "the universe" was similar to those with religious beliefs of leaving things "to God." Essentially, we were saying the same thing, just crediting a different source. All this time, I'd been thinking that people were idiots for believing their God is right when maybe they merely wanted to believe that something more powerful than them exists. Maybe the exact title we put on the powerful thing was less important than having the ability to breathe and let go of shit.

As a classic overthinker, I started to wonder - why was all this woo-woo shit coming into my life right now? Of course, my mind strayed back to my doctor in the U.S. and the pending biopsy results. At first, my mind went to the worst-case scenario. "That's it, I'm dying, and I needed to come to peace before I leave the earth!" my overly dramatic brain told me. But I felt too calm for that to be real. Maybe, just maybe, this was coming into my life at this exact moment so that I could take steps toward healing my body myself. Maybe I should be more kind and loving to myself and forgive others for whatever things I'd been carrying around inside me while it slowly poisoned me. Buddha is quoted as saying, "Holding on to anger is like drinking poison and expecting the other person to die." Certainly, I'd been drinking that kind of poison for years since I was not the type to let shit go. Perhaps my blood was full of emotional toxicity. My analysis started to overwhelm me with possibilities, so I decided to focus my meditations on only one thing: healing my body.

There was one meditation that I found super enjoyable; it walked me through visualizing a blue light transmitting through my body and healing things as I went. It was easy enough for me to imagine pulling this blue light from the earth up through my feet and allowing it to pinball through my veins. My imagination conjured up a Pac-Man-like light that gobbled up extra platelets in the blood and restored good health. This became my go-to meditation each night before bed, and I completed it religiously. Not that anything changed that I could tell. My sleep was good, and I found that meditating was easier than I previously thought. My brain often wandered off, but eventually, I found my way back, and I always felt better at the end than before I started.

Everything else sort of became a blur outside of my self-healing routines. Of course, I worked during the day. In Peru, the time zones are closely aligned to the U.S., so it wasn't as easy to check out the local landscape during the day. There was enough time to squeeze in walking breaks throughout the day to remind myself how lucky I was to be working from this remote location. Some days, I would bring my laptop to the restaurant for lunch and sit overlooking the ocean; this view definitely wasn't available at home in Phoenix. If I had my face stuffed in a laptop, who cares if there was an ocean just beyond? Because when I took a break and looked up out

159

of the uninterrupted wall of windows, I saw the dark blue-black of the ocean and would unconsciously take a deep breath and breathe out slowly. Without knowing it, I was building a gratitude practice.

After Grace left Peru, I opened my e-mail to a message titled "MEDITATE BITCH." Included was a bunch of information on meditation, including recommendations for books to read, movies to watch, and people to follow. This was a woo-woo treasure trove that allowed me to jump in at a much higher level sooner than I would have been able to do on my own. Sure, I would have eventually come across some of the information or experts that Grace recommended. But who knows if I would have taken this practice as seriously if I wasn't exposed to such excellent information early in the process.

With so much time alone on my hands, I buckled down and dove into the material. This unexpected full leap into the woo-woo world of vegetarianism (yep, I quit meat after the juice cleanse...it simply felt right), yoga, and meditation provided a canvas for learning. My appetite for information was voracious and pushed out any FOMO I may have had about what the other digital nomads were doing: making fast friends, going on sandboarding trips down the mountains of Peru, or starting up new businesses while scrunched in around the community table at the co-working space. My full attention was consumed with learning and practicing.

My work days had always been crazy, probably self-imposed, because I was horrible at setting boundaries, but I also liked the feeling of working hard. Or maybe it was the feeling of being busy that was an addiction. During the days in Miraflores, outside of Lima, I started adding breaks during the day to walk along the Malecón. This simple act of self-love, detaching myself from my computer, allowed my anxieties to settle and introduced me to a more balanced mind.

As I began to look forward to my walks, it became easier to detach from my laptop. I mean, who wouldn't want to detach in this location? Yes, Lima had the hazy gray film that tends to hang around most ocean-side landscapes in a mild climate. The dew point was higher than I was used to, being from the dry desert, but the majestic cliffs overlooking the black water of the Pacific Ocean were soothing and energizing, all at the same time. Sunlight would peek through the cloud cover and sometimes burned off the haze entirely, but it was never cold. The temperature was always a warm-cool, probably due to the high humidity. The ocean was excruciatingly cold, though, and the beaches full of stones and pebbles, so I stuck with walking at the top of the cliffs along the paved Malecón woven with parks, playgrounds, coffee kiosks, and even a mall.

It was certainly more crowded up on the cliffs, but I would put my headphones in and turn on the custom playlist I created on Spotify. Something was shifting in me because gangster rap had always been my favorite go-to music, but now my playlist was full of modern, jazzy, pop-style music (if that's not a genre yet, it should be). Messages like "Fuck the Police" were replaced with "Her Life" by Two Feet. Prior to Peru, I'd never even heard of Two Feet, but sometimes messages reach you serendipitously. While in an Uber, I heard a song and fell in love with all of it: the jazzy sound, the lure of his voice, and the perfectly crafted lyrics. I became obsessed with the sounds and saved every song I could find. My favorite was clear the moment I heard it because it's as if he wrote the song specifically for me. It was short and simple but incredibly accurate:

> *Every day she sees her life*
> *Fade away, and pass her by*
> *What can she do?*
> *Wants to leave her lonely town*
> *Wants to go and fuck around*
> *What can she do?*
> *It's her life*
> *Wants to quit all of her jobs*
> *Sell her house and move along*
> *What can she do?*
> *Lives in dreams and self-told lies*
> *Sees the world through jaded eyes*
> *What can she do?*
> *It's her life*

The lyrics resonated with me on such a deep level because it felt so true. Seriously, *get out of my head, dude!* Had you asked me prior to travel if I was miserable and needed an escape, I would have answered no. But looking back at the rinse, repeat quality of life I had before traveling, I felt so enlightened.

This was a breaking of the chains that held me to my previous life, the self-imposed rules that told me I had to work in a certain type of role, or date a certain type of person, or own a home. Had I never left my old life, I would have been worried about what career move to take next, to prove I was capable and still climbing the ladder. My evenings would have been full of networking events or bottles of wine (or both). My wardrobe would have to be updated for said events, and I would have felt pressure to upgrade my car, my house, my body for fear of judgment from others. Travel provided an escape from the requirements and expectations of society. And more than that, it was a clear message to my head and heart that I was capable of far more than I thought I was.

During the last three weeks, I took a moment to give myself props, which was fairly rare inside my always critical mind. When my prior excuse would have been, *I don't have time*; here I was proving to myself that I did have time. I was working full-time while in another country, exploring new places and navigating new things, and I still had time to begin exercising again. Not just exercise, but I'd now taken yoga in Spanish when before, my lack of knowledge of poses would have prevented me from attending a session in English. Then, there was the slightly failed, but at least attempted, juice cleanse. Oh, and my nightly meditation. That's a lot of change in three weeks' time. As I moved into my fourth week, I resolved to keep it up, even though this final week I'd be shaking up my routine with a week of vacation to make the short trip to the Sacred Valley, where I'd be visiting the famed Machu Picchu.

♥

Machu Picchu

Back when I was living with the sociopath, er...I mean Tom, we used to watch *Extreme Makeover: Weight Loss Edition* (remember that reality show with Chris Powell?). One episode featured a prize trip to Machu Picchu, and I was fascinated by the beauty that had radiated from the TV screen and imprinted on my brain. This was a place I *had* to visit, I decided. I copied a picture online and put it as my Facebook cover photo so that I would continue to see it and visualize myself visiting there. At that point in time, my international travel only included Mexico and Canada, aside from a few vacations to various islands in the Caribbean. Not exactly what you would call 'well-traveled' or adventurous. Tom reluctantly agreed that he would go with me, but since he would only fly first class, the trip was out of reach due to the extraordinary expense. Not to mention he didn't like to travel anywhere that he didn't speak the language. At the time, I could never comprehend that nuance, but after I learned of his deceitful ways, it made more sense - how could you con people if you couldn't communicate? Thankfully, we never made that trip; it would have ruined the experience for me. Funny how everything always happens for a reason. Sometimes, it doesn't make sense in the moment, so all you can do is trust the process.

But now, my waiting was finally over! I had scheduled this final week in Peru as vacation so I could tour the Sacred Valley, starting in Cusco and ending at Machu Picchu. This had been a long time coming, and I couldn't wait to see the beautiful Inca monument. As soon as we landed in Cusco, we were met by older women in traditional costumes, their dark hair braided and deep lines etched into their skin, and they offered small baggies of dried leaves for sale. These were no ordinary leaves; they were coca leaves (the precursor to cocaine) that help cure altitude sickness. We just landed at over 11,000 feet, so nausea, headaches, dizziness, and fatigue were common symptoms for newcomers. Isn't it beautiful how nature works? There is a leaf you can chew to help ease the symptoms, rather than popping a chemical cocktail that Acme Pharmaceutical swears is the only cure. Those of us affected by the height started chewing on leaves immediately and continued to drink the tea for the first couple of days into our trip. Our first few days consisted of a bus trip that wound us through the picturesque countryside of the Sacred Valley, and we ended in Urubamba. From there, the train took us the rest of the way to Aguas Calientes, the tiny town at the base of Machu Picchu. We stayed there the night before our hike so we could catch the bus up the mountain to the entrance first thing in the morning.

Have I mentioned I'm deathly afraid of heights? This trek might end in a panic attack on my part, but I was determined to see the sights. After the horrible bus ride up, I was a little nervous about what may come next. The road the bus traveled was a twisting turning single lane up the hill, with the bus traveling at rates of speed that couldn't have been safe, especially considering that the road was shared with the empty buses headed back down to pick up more passengers. By the time we escaped what could have been our giant metal coffin, I was white-knuckled and practicing some deep breathing Lamaze that I didn't even realize I remembered from birthing my daughter over 20 years ago.

Underwhelmed. That's how I felt in the gravel parking lot at the top of the mountain. Buses were whirring by, and it smelled of exhaust fumes. Crowds of tourists were everywhere, clogging the ability to appreciate the beautiful stone walls or lush vegetation. My teeth chattered as we stood amidst the damp fog in a group waiting for our guide while one of our group mates tried to resolve an issue with their ticket to get accepted through the main gate. Machu Picchu had become such a tourist attraction that the number of tickets was limited to restrict the foot traffic on the trails and through the Incan ruins. These tickets had to be purchased relatively far in advance and were designated for a specific day, either in the morning or afternoon. I'm not sure exactly what I expected since my only real knowledge was based on the one view we see in all the pictures. You know, the one with the mountains rising behind the ancient city ruins, taken from far above. Maybe that photo was taken with a drone and I wouldn't actually get to experience that for myself. Had I traveled all this way only to find out the pictures online far exceeded the location in person? That had happened so many times already…photos taken by drones plague the internet, causing people to flock to the location, only to find it looks nothing like expected when you are standing on foot. Sometimes the internet's a bitch.

We finally got through the gate and started moving along our path. The guide provided all kinds of insight and information along the way, but the path was nothing like I'd expected. My research had indicated I would need hiking boots, cold weather gear, and Frog Toggs due to the unpredictable rain. My backpack was prepared for a rough hike, but we were walking along a well-established trail that had been around for centuries. Stones were stacked so neatly that it made you wonder how 15th-century Incas had the ingenuity and ability to construct them. The lush greenness of the hillsides appeared perfectly manicured, and we stopped the first few times we encountered llamas along the trail, intermingling with people and seemingly posing for their picture to be taken.

We were taking the path to the Sun Gate, or Inti Punku, a pass used to allow people in or out of the fortress back in the day. Since we were hiking up in the morning, there were low-hanging clouds everywhere, and as we ascended, it looked kind of like we were entering heaven (if I believed in heaven). At first, I was disappointed, thinking I wouldn't get to see the idyllic view of the fortress below through all those clouds. Everyone wanted to have their own recognizable photo of the Machu Picchu you see online and in movies. But at 8:00 am this February morning, everything was a swirl of gray. There was no sun in the sky, and we couldn't see far up the trail or down the mountainside we recently came from. Before I spun off into a downhearted spiral, I looked around to truly appreciate the view of the clouds. If I wiped away my expectations about getting one photo of one particular view, I wouldn't be disappointed by the actual view in front of me at all. It was stunning. Majestic. The mountainsides were vibrant green, with heavy clouds sitting on their shoulders. I breathed in the crisp air and allowed the surreal view to change my attitude.

 The rest of the way to the Sun Gate was spent trying to snap as many photos of the clouds as possible. Not surprisingly, the actual Sun Gate wasn't much to see. It was a pass that allowed a view of both sides of the mountain, but with the visibility as it were, I couldn't see much. As we headed down toward the ruins to hear more about how the Inca people lived within the fortress, I resigned myself to not seeing the view I had hoped to capture. The blue sky was starting to peek through the clouds, and the temperature warmed enough for me to remove my jacket. The cloud cover was burning off and I wanted to run back up the hill to see if I could get the photos I thought I would have snapped from the Sun Gate. Until we rounded a corner on the trail, and from there, the ruins were clear and it looked exactly like it did on the internet, but in real life. Apparently, this was the spot the ruins were visible from - not the topmost vantage point of the Sun Gate, but along the trail between the Sun Gate and the ruins.

Huayna Picchu mountain was jutting up in the distance behind the ruins, with its rocky cap dusted with wisps of clouds. Below it sat a few smaller peaks covered in lush green vegetation. Sprawled out beneath those peaks were the zig zag stone walls of the ruins laid out on the green flooring that once was the citadel. The view did not disappoint; it was actually so much better in person that it made me giddy. Everyone was buzzing with excitement as they took video, photos, and selfies from this vantage point. This felt like *the* moment. If we were going to experience magic, it would be in this glorious spot right here.

Why would anyone expect magic in Machu Picchu? Well, the little research I had done prior to trekking all the way down here indicated there was a special energy here. It's one of the sacred sites on earth believed to be an energy vortex. Since my journey into the woo-woo world had only begun a few weeks ago, I didn't know what an energy vortex was or what it was supposed to do to you. Honestly, since I grew up an hour from one of the well-known vortices in Sedona, Arizona, I didn't place much on the reality of encountering anything special. I'd been to Sedona dozens of times and never felt any "energy" or experienced any of the magic that seemed expected. Though my cynicism didn't stop me from trying to find the Sun Dial once we were within the Inca city walls. Based on what I read, the Sun Dial was supposed to hold incredible energy, which people can actually feel when they touch it. So naturally, I wanted to touch it. Not that I was expecting to feel anything, but I was looking for reasons *not* to believe this is possible.

It was probably broken now anyway, I mused, after reading that some asshat filmed a beer commercial here, and the crane fell on the rock, breaking it. Seriously, what the fuck is wrong with the world? Now we are filming fucking beer commercials at Unesco Heritage sites? Can't we photoshop a picture of the beer in, rather than destroy what took hordes of ancient people years to build? Sometimes, I'm embarrassed to be part of the human race. Yet, here I was, being a tourist like everyone else, so I guess I couldn't shirk my own humanity.

Our guide weaved us between different fascinating points of interest, demonstrating things like how the Inca got water. He came to a structure that he said is believed to be a worship site due to the perfection in the construction of the stone. It was true; the stone blocks here couldn't have been more perfect had they been cut with modern-day machinery. How was it possible that people living hundreds of years ago, with crude tools and no modern-day technology, built this? Maybe that was the *real* magic of this place, the sheer awe and wonder of the majestic effort it would have taken to construct this fortress.

The Sun Dial found me by accident. Our guided tour ended, and we were left with some time to explore on our own, take additional pictures, and hang out with the llamas until our morning pass expired. As I wandered around, I saw some steps leading up to what looked like a stone platform. There was a short line going up, but it appeared to be moving quickly, so I joined them and noticed that this spot was marked as the Sun Dial. It wasn't what I was expecting at all, just a chunk of stone. Once we reached the platform at the top of the steps, I was disappointed to find that ropes were blocking off the stone dial, and a man in full uniform was standing guard. He kept the line moving so each person had time for a quick photo as they walked by, but absolutely no one could *touch* the stone. Of course, given my rant about how humans suck and they ruin everything, I agreed with this policy. But my shoulders still slumped in disappointment since I was still human and wanted to touch it, to see if anything magical happened.

The dial looked almost like a headstone, jutting up from a boulder that appeared more naturally attached to the mountain. It all seemed to be one stone that probably had its roots deep underneath the surface. As I approached, I started snapping shots with my iPhone since I wouldn't have time to linger with the line being encouraged to *keep moving*. As I tapped, tapped, tapped on my camera, I felt something. Right as I passed the square, flat surface of the bottom boulder with the dial jutting up from it, there was a quivering in my chest. Certainly, I must have hesitated, but I kept one foot moving in front of the next, and once I passed the stone, the feeling abruptly stopped. Did I imagine the whole thing? Most definitely not.

The vibration I felt in my chest snapped me right back to memories from high school. We used to build speaker boxes and put them in the trunk of our cars so that we could cruise around on Friday and Saturday nights with our bass thumping out all the best rap tunes from the late 1980s and early 1990s. Inside the car, you would feel the thud, thud, thud of the bass pounding, but even when other cars would pass by you, you could feel the reverberations of the bass shake inside your body. That was exactly what it felt like when I walked by the Sun Dial: like a pimped-out 1988 Nissan Sentra just rolled by, bumping some NWA. Except there were no cars here in the ruins. Which was probably good because NWA in a sacred ruin would most likely be frowned upon.

Inside my brain, thoughts were running a mile a minute. If I felt that sensation in my chest, it had to come from somewhere. My mind was blown by the idea that an energy vortex might be a real thing. Even with my current exploration of all the woo-woo stuff, part of my brain was trying to argue away the concept that we are somehow all connected energetically in the universe. It's completely logical that there would be energy vortexes; after all, we get all of our electricity from the earth. Didn't I watch the documentary on Tesla and Einstein? But if I believed this to be true, didn't that make me more of a tie-dye-wearing hippie than a suit jacket and heels corporate America type that I had strived so hard to become?

My perception of what was real was changing, which ironically pulled me more inside my own head. I no longer cared about walking around the ruins. I had seen what I had come to see, and now I wanted time to think. Since childhood, I'd been fighting the concept of religion, which for me included spirituality. By the time I was old enough to separate the dogma of religion from the mysticism of spirituality, I'd shunned any related topic and looked no deeper. Not only did I not look, but I actively fought to keep anything that sounded remotely religious out of my periphery. I had learned to hate what it symbolized. What had my sweeping generalization of religion cost me? *The ability to believe in something larger than myself and the hope that this life meant something more than mere existence.*

My time in the park hadn't quite expired yet, but I walked back to the bus stop to catch the bus back down the hill. After a small wait in line for the bus, I was jolted out of my reverie as the bus lurched forward and started the descent. If I thought the ride up was horrendous, it was merely a warm-up for the ride down. The narrow road had the bus hugging the edge of the cliff. All morning, I'd avoided any of my fear of heights, but now I sat in the window seat looking down...off the side of the cliff. I couldn't even see a pinch of road next to the bus tires; we were so close to the road's edge to allow for the traffic heading up the other side. My stomach was rolling around, and I'd never been more grateful that I hadn't eaten in hours. Deep breathing didn't help calm my nerves since the bus driver was clearly driving way too fast for these conditions. As I peered around the bus at the other passengers, I saw many of them gripping the headrest in front of them. Then, there were the complete psychopaths who appeared utterly unphased by this death trip down the mountain. In that moment, I decided there was no way to avoid my motion sickness, so rather than try to focus on a spot out the window, I bent my body forward and put my head in my lap. Certain that I looked completely ridiculous to the stranger that accompanied the seat next to me, I resigned myself to it and focused on my breath. If this bus launched off the side of the mountain, at least I'd be the last to know.

Surprisingly, we made it to the bottom unscathed. Possibly, it was the near-death experience I had on the bus, or maybe the realization that there was more to the earth and energy than I had ever speculated, but I didn't have the mental energy to spend time around any other humans. My appetite returned after I walked around a bit, so I got something to eat and then popped into some shops alone, lost in my thoughts. In two days, I would leave this group and fly to Colombia alone, so I had to get used to being alone. Shopping alone. Eating alone. Thinking alone.

We boarded the train that was taking us out of the Sacred Valley and back to Cusco for a quick flight back to Lima. Shortly into the trip, the train got stuck on the tracks, delayed due to a train accident somewhere further down the tracks. Other members of the group I was traveling with started to play games to pass the time, but I was still in my mood from earlier in the day. I wished the train and everyone on it would disappear so I could be alone with my thoughts. I was certain everyone in the group thought I was a complete bitch, which usually would bother me, but I no longer cared. I was so exhausted from trying to make small talk with people I didn't know. My thoughts were deep and took me on twists and turns around the possibilities in the universe. Instead of trying to fit in and blend with the hangry and bored crowd on the train, I inserted my headphones in my ears and turned on one of the meditations Grace sent me. It seemed there was no better time to close my eyes and turn my attention inward.

♥

Colombia

My flight to Medellín, Colombia, departed from Lima a few hours after I returned from Machu Picchu. As I checked in for my flight, the woman at the ticket counter asked me how long I would be staying in Colombia. Not an uncommon question, considering I was flying on a one-way ticket, but I'd never had anyone actually question me. So I told her I would be in the country for one month and expected her to check my bag and move along. Instead, she questioned me further. "Do you have a return flight booked? If so, I need to see your flight reservation." I told her I didn't have a flight reservation, but I would make sure to leave in one month's time. She looked at me like I was stupid - *how dare I think I can come and go as I please*? Honestly, I had read about this online and there were lots of tips and tricks to avoid purchasing tickets in advance. Supposedly, there were websites where you could put a ticket on hold but never pay for it so that you could skate by overzealous ticketing agents or customs agents. I hadn't taken it that seriously since I'd never been asked about my departing flights, and certainly never been asked to show proof. Of all the countries I'd been to thus far, I would never have guessed I'd be denied entry to Colombia. The country that didn't even have a postal system had its shit together enough to require a solo American woman to show proof she is going to get the fuck out.

Anyway, the agent refused to check my bag until I provided proof of my scheduled departure, so I got out of line and frantically started searching for flights on a discount app. My itinerary was still up in the air at that point, and I wasn't ready to make a decision for a month down the road, but I had decided to keep moving north into Central America. The weather is warmer there, and there are plenty of small towns that suit my introverted ways. There was a super cool place in Costa Rica that I'd heard about. You live in treehouses on the property, and in exchange for the prepared meals you receive, you help tend to the gardens. I was also thinking about a little surf village in Nicaragua that was well-known in the digital nomad circle. Without having time to do more research, I booked a one-way ticket from Colombia to Costa Rica and got back in line so I wouldn't miss my flight to Medellín.

The Costa Rica ticket was a little more expensive than anticipated, but it allowed me to board my flight, so I was temporarily sated. While I waited for my flight, I figured I'd firm up my reservations for the next few months so I wouldn't get stuck in this position again. As I reviewed the requirements for traveling from Colombia to Costa Rica, I found that a vaccination for Yellow Fever was required. Previously, I missed this detail because the requirements change depending on the country you are coming from and weren't required from the U.S. Even if I were a fan of vaccines, it would be a logistical challenge to find a place in Medellín that could get me in with enough time before my exit from the country. I felt it was a bit of an oxymoron to inject myself with who knows what in a vaccine to gain access to an all-natural farming community in Costa Rica. In 'fly by the seat of my pants' fashion, I completely pivoted and searched Guatemala. There was a small apartment available in

Antigua for $500 for the entire month. $500 bucks for the whole month! If I booked here instead of Costa Rica, I wouldn't need any vaccine, and the low rent made up for the fact that I would lose the non-refundable airline ticket. Done. Booked. While I was at it, I decided to book the next leg and searched Nicaragua, found a great apartment, and booked. Wondering if my free-spirited attitude would diminish if I had my destinations for the next three months planned out, I hesitated momentarily. Then I decided, fuck it, this didn't diminish anything, and immediately booked and paid for both. It felt pretty damn good knowing I was heading to all these places solo. I was ready for the adventures to begin!

♥

Going Solo

The sky was dark, and the airport was sparsely populated when I landed in Medellín. Since I suspected the airport wouldn't be brimming with people at 11:00 pm, I had booked my transportation in advance. A car would pick me up and make the drive down the zig-zag road through the jungle between the airport and the neighborhood in Medellín, where the guards at my new apartment were available to let me in 24/7. There was so much hype about how dangerous Columbia was, but I jutted my chin out in stubborn defiance and refused to accept the rumors as fact. Despite that, there was a little rumble of nervousness in my gut, being a solo female wandering around outside the airport late at night. Relief washed over me when I found my bilingual driver, but that was short-lived when he told me he had arranged for another driver to take me into town due to a family emergency he needed to get to. Uneasily, I got into the car with the new driver, who spoke no English. Something I had been working on, practicing really, was trusting in the general good of people. But that didn't stop me from putting my apartment address in Google Maps and tracking my little blue dot, just to make sure we were headed in the right direction. Ordinarily, my resting bitch face ensured that most strangers provided a wide berth, like they had encountered a rattlesnake and were trying to avoid the strike zone. This was a great defense mechanism for walking down crowded streets in Europe but didn't provide much comfort when trapped in the backseat of a moving vehicle in South America. Fortunately, he proved to just be a driver doing his job. He deposited me in front of the apartment complex without harming a hair on my head.

 Arriving in the cloak of night, the beauty of this city in the jungle didn't make itself apparent until morning. Once the day broke, I could see the rolling hills full of lush green from my apartment on the 8th floor. Quickly, I showered and got dressed while silently patting myself on the back for picking out this modern apartment with an amazing view of the populated jungle city. While still on the apartment Wi-Fi I downloaded an offline map since I couldn't pick up a SIM card at the airport due to my late-night arrival. It was a Sunday, so I had nothing on the agenda for the day. All I wanted to do was walk around and get acquainted with this neighborhood. And find some breakfast. I realized I was starving and had no food in the fridge yet. Wandering the streets, I made a note of restaurants and coffee shops I would like to come back to. It was strange to think that I wouldn't be meeting up with any groups or travel friends this time. In Colombia, I was truly alone for real.

All.

By.

Myself.

What was the longest amount of time I had ever truly spent alone? Before Europe, I had spent a few weekends working, drinking wine and watching Netflix, not leaving the house except for occasional necessary food. But that was at home where I could always call friends or family to come over, had I not wanted to be alone. In Europe, I had spent the weekend in Vigo, Spain. Sure, there were plenty of times I had walked around, exploring on my own. But there was always the promise of going back to my apartment and chatting with Emma or Grace while they whipped up something on the stove. I'd stand there useless in the kitchen, drinking wine or maybe doing dishes since that's the safest contribution I could provide. I'd never been much of a cook, though I could put together something edible if I tried. But I hate it. The whole process, really. Picking menus, grocery shopping, food prepping, paying attention while I stir things on the stove, trying to identify if the temperature is satisfactory for properly eliminating any food borne parasites. But washing dishes I could handle. And pouring wine. How many European evenings were spent this way before we all scattered off to our individual rooms to finish our work day in the North American time zones?

Alone. I wasn't truly alone that often in Europe. But here, in Medellín, I walked the sloping neighborhoods, and it sunk in that my list of places I wanted to see here, I'd be coming back to by myself. There would be no option to meet Grace or Emma for coffee or to go back to my apartment and chat with a roommate. I wondered if I would get bored having dinner conversations with myself every night. Coffee for one. Lunch for one. Dinner for one. At least I wouldn't have to worry if anyone else would like the places I'd selected to eat. As I walked and thought, my heart rate accelerated, and in my mind, I started to panic. Could I handle being all alone? I'd already walked around the square in the neighborhood and was bored. What was I going to do with myself, by myself, for months? Maybe I should go home early. Yes, I could always go home; that didn't sound horrible. My feet kept moving, up one street, down another. My mind raced and I determined I absolutely could *not* go home early. What a stupid idea! I just needed to acclimate to being alone. I could do this. I would do this. Perhaps I might bore myself to tears, but I needed to find out what happened if I only had myself to listen to. My pulse returned to normal, and I started to pay attention to my surroundings again. There were some cute shops selling local goods that I could see on display through the windows, but they weren't open early on a Sunday morning. When I saw a place serving pancakes, I ducked in and asked for a table for one in my broken Spanglish. This wasn't so bad. Dining alone felt much better once I'd consumed pancakes and coffee. With my tummy full and my anxiety abated, I continued my exploration of this new city.

Tucked away on the bottom floor of a shopping mall, I ran across the cleanest yoga studio I'd ever seen. Most Bikram studios that I had been to smelled like a cross between cat piss and dirty feet. This one was pristine and odor-free. When I checked the class schedule, it appeared my work schedule was going to interfere with most of the classes I wanted to take. Unless I wanted to get up at the crack of dawn, which I was no longer accustomed to, nor did I have any desire to make the 30-minute walk alone in the darkness of the pre-dawn hours. No one in the studio could understand my questions in mangled Spanish, so I took the pamphlet and continued my exploration of the city.

For the next couple of days, I kept that pamphlet affixed to the fridge door with a magnet, trying to figure out a way to escape work for two hours in the middle of the day. A few days after my arrival in Colombia, an escape was provided. When my phone rang, and I saw the name pop up for the CFO of our investor group, I knew what was happening. We had been struggling with revenue for a while, and even with me stepping aside to allow more qualified people to run the sales and operations aspects, we were doing worse than ever. It was so bad one of our sister companies had loaned us a salesperson who had come up with some knee-jerk, last-ditch ideas to try to generate revenue. Those ideas were a bad deal for everyone involved, and I had cautioned that we were over-promising with a guarantee of under-delivering. My concerns were maybe half-heard, and I couldn't blame anyone for wanting to take the gamble. They had listened to me long enough without the desired results on our P&L.

Now, I knew I was receiving the call that the company was shutting its doors. Officially out of money, ideas, and confidence in our team. I took a deep breath and answered the call cheerfully, trying to make his job as easy as possible. I'd terminated enough people to know that regardless of reason, it was never easy. Unless you're a psychopath who enjoys hurting people for your own pleasure. His voice sounded relieved when I told him I understood. He had HR for the parent company on the line, and she piped in and asked where she could mail my severance paperwork. I'd never met this woman before, but she sounded like your standard HR robot. When I asked if she could e-mail me the paperwork for electronic signature, she replied with a firm "no." "Well, you may have trouble mailing it to me. There is no postal system where I am," I told her. She must have thought I was bullshitting her when she incredulously asked,

"Where are you?" Interesting, I thought. They must not have told her I was working remotely. That seems like a weird omission. "I'm in Colombia. They don't have a postal system in this country, so I can't receive mail. I have perfectly good Wi-Fi though." She reluctantly agreed to e-mail me the documents and accepted a scanned copy of the signed version, which was a relief. Not that they were offering much of a package, but anything to help get me through a few more weeks was appreciated. I've never been a great saver of money, so my rainy-day funds were pretty limited.

Our entire team was let go that day, effective immediately. All the time and effort I had exerted to try to build something successful, and this was the final evidence of being a complete failure. *I had failed.* Not that I was surprised. Isn't that what I had expected to happen? What my evil inside voice had whispered to me time and time again?

"You don't know what you are doing."

"You are an imposter."

"What makes you think you can set up a successful agency?"

That voice drove me to California and told me that other, more experienced people could do it better than me. But that was all bullshit, as our evil inside voice usually is. My involvement didn't single-handedly make the company fail; there were about a hundred other valid reasons why it didn't work out. Still, I couldn't shake the guilt and responsibility I felt for the final outcome.

As I sat at my cozy Colombian kitchen counter, I placed my cell phone on the smooth white surface and stared at it. What the hell was I supposed to do now? Finding a job while in Colombia seemed impossible, but going back home to look for work this early into my South America adventure seemed even more impossible...for my soul. If I left now, would I ever have the chance to complete my travels in the future? What if I died before I had this kind of freedom again? If I stayed here, the dynamics of my solo travel were bound to change. I would have no daily calls or LinkedIn messages to keep me connected to other people. I would actually be cloaked in solitude. While that was scary, it was something I didn't realize I desperately needed.

As I tried to think of something positive, I realized that this was my sign that manifestation was real; I wanted time to take my yoga classes, and now I had time. Rather than try to solve the employment issue immediately, I gave myself the next three weeks in Colombia to feel it out. Instead of my usual days full of internet stalking and phone calls, there was plenty of time for activities. The first thing I did was return to the yoga studio and prepaid for a couple of weeks' worth of classes. Money was a resource I wanted to conserve, so I only selected two tourist activities to help fill my time. One was a coffee-picking and roasting tour, and the other would take me to a giant rock I had seen in a photo once. Without work to distract me, I wondered what would happen to my sanity. I still had a couple of months to make it through, and I didn't have the resources to occupy my time with a bunch of expensive activities.

On the day of the coffee plantation tour, a group met outside the tour office in town and piled into jeeps equipped to handle off-road terrain. The jeeps thrust us deep into the lush jungle surrounding Medellín, which was surprisingly close to the neighborhood where I was staying. I had expected to drive for quite some time in order to get into this dense of jungle, with supple plants providing a canopy so thick I felt like I was in a movie. Except in the movies, there was always some type of predator lurking beyond the bright green leaves. For us, we had the less ominous experience of picking coffee beans on the rolling hills. We arrived at a family farm where they showed us how to dry the beans we picked and then demonstrated all the stages involved in roasting the beans and how it impacts the flavor of the coffee we consume. Most importantly, our group was able to sample all the different roasts to experience the changing flavors depending on the heat level and time exposed to that temperature. Outside on the large porch overlooking the jungle, the family served an incredible lunch filled with local cuisine. Our tummies were full as we climbed back in the jeeps to 4-wheel down the muddy roads since it had started drizzling.

Something I had learned in Medellín was to prepare for the drizzle. Especially since I walked everywhere, I had to take my rain jacket with me every time I left the house. Certainly different than in Arizona, where I might use a raincoat once per year, here I was using it every day. I'd leave my apartment with my backpack on my back, raincoat tucked into a pocket. And I'd return with my backpack on backward, so my laptop was protected against my belly, with the raincoat on and zipped up, making it look like I was halfway through a pregnancy.

Without work to worry about, I didn't have to carry my laptop around any longer, and instead, I went to yoga most days. The classes were fully in Spanish, but the flow was the same as the Bikram classes I had taken years earlier. Quickly, I was back in the routine of the movements…not that I was any good. Occasionally, I'd find myself doing something wrong, but once I saw everyone else in the class moving into a different pose, I'd quickly correct my movement, always a few seconds lag time behind everyone else. At home, I'd be embarrassed if that happened, somehow expecting myself to always be perfect. Here, I was learning to cut myself some slack. Although I did feel my face flush one day when the instructor was repeatedly saying something in Spanish and finally walked over to me to correct my form. But after a quick breath into the pose, I let go of the perfectionist expectation that I would be able to respond to a correction given in a language I don't even speak. Isn't it ridiculous the expectations we set for ourselves sometimes?

There was a certain freedom to scheduling my tour of El Peñón de Guatapé (the big rock I mentioned) during the middle of the week. It was different than being on vacation. This felt like an exercise in doing whatever the fuck I wanted, and I could imagine how addicting that might be. It was a day-long bus tour that stopped in a few small towns, sampling the local cuisine and viewing some landmarks. Honestly, I could have skipped over stopping in the little towns. Being alone in these situations where we killed time shopping and eating together as a group only made me more uncomfortable than had we gotten straight to the point of the tour. Surely, other normal people enjoyed this aspect, *especially* if they were alone, because they would have friends by the time they reached Guatapé. But not me. Small talk was my worst nightmare, and I didn't speak the local language anyway. Some of the people on the tour spoke English and they sounded like they were from some exciting places, but I couldn't bring myself to talk to strangers. I don't know if it's crippling shyness or the fact that I simply don't care about strangers enough to ask them questions about where they are from or what their life is like. I've always wondered if most other people actually care about that shit when they ask. Or do they engage in the process of speaking to another human because they're so uncomfortable with silence? Like, why do you care where I'm from or do for a living when you don't even know me? I'd rather hear nothing than have to nod my head, pretending to be interested as someone shares their reason for coming on this trip. I don't even know you; why should I care that your ex-girlfriend is from

Colombia and so you've always dreamed of coming here in some weird, stalker-y way? Perhaps I'm nothing but an excessive level of a self-absorbed asshole who only cares what's going on inside my own head, not other people's.

The highlight of the bus tour was a stop to climb the famous El Peñón de Guatapé, which is essentially the biggest rock I'd ever seen, kind of shaped like a giant Easter egg. It was well worth the 656 steps up to the top, which earned a view of amazingly turquoise pools of water that surrounded the giant rock. There were channels of lakes as far as I could see, rolling hills of green sloping down to the water's edge, with houses peppered alongside the water. What a treat it must be for those who live here to wake up every day and breathe this air and their gaze taking in the lush greenery reflecting off the blue waters. Do they appreciate it? Or do they take it for granted like we tend to do with most things we see every day?

Maybe that was the novelty of traveling. Not seeing the same thing every day provided a canvas for appreciation. Before I left Phoenix, I'd become numb to the beauty of the desert. The light greens and browns of the scrub brush on the roadside would blend into the deep tans of the hard desert floor. All I could think as I drove around my hometown was bleh. Did the locals near El Peñol think this glorious view was bleh? Because I thought it was magnificent. Before loading back on the bus, I sat in the parking lot oblivious to everyone around me, drinking in the colors of greens and blues that surrounded me. Not only did I start understanding the importance of travel, but there was also a swell of appreciation deep in my chest that my schedule was cleared, allowing me to even be here in the middle of the week. Would I have booked this tour if I was still working? That remains unknown, but all I could do was appreciate the current moment and sit with it until we headed back to Medellín.

♥

Should I Stay or Go?

On the surface, it felt as though there was nothing earth-shattering that happened in Colombia. Sometimes, though, what seems insignificant in the moment turns out to be the most pivotal point on our journey. For the most part, I mainly spent a lot of ordinary moments that added up to an inordinate amount of time with myself. My Spanish wasn't great, and even if it were, my introvertedness would have prevented me from venturing out and talking to complete strangers anyway. My time spent touring, sitting at coffee shops, or meandering between shops and restaurants was essentially time alone with my thoughts. It didn't take long to recognize I had been given a great gift. Often, when we are faced with a big decision, we aren't provided any extra time to evaluate our options, the consequences, or anything in between. It was like the time when I learned that Tom was up to something, but I didn't know what. There was no time then to hash out the details, I had to decide and take action. Back in Colombia, there was a lot of fear rolling around in my head because I was neither independently wealthy nor prepared to live without income for an extended period of time. However, I knew that if I went home to hit the pavement looking for work, I would probably never make it back to South America, and I would miss out on whatever lesson I was in the process of learning down here by myself. I had to accept my new reality. This would not be the first time, nor the last, that I would have to create a new reality and accept that my prior life was not my future life. I think that's an interesting skill I'd never fully appreciated or even noticed. Most people delay making big decisions, cutting bad people out of their lives, or doing other hard things because it means they have to accept a new reality. You could witness this any given day on the news, where a mother of a criminal was interviewed in full protest of the facts; "not *my* baby." Her opinion of her offspring had been formed, and she wasn't willing to change the narrative she wanted to believe, because it was just too painful. But each time I had accepted that my universe had been shattered, I recreated it a little bit better, hadn't I?

Much like the process of being by myself was a skill I hadn't fully mastered yet, but I was getting better at it. When I first arrived, I found that my excursions out of my apartment were short. I'd venture out for one purpose, like eating lunch, and then head straight back to home base to ponder what to do next. Like a dog that has been rescued from the pound, who will only timidly set one paw inside your home. Honestly, it was probably the fact that my apartment was at the top of a steep hill that got me to reconsider this process. My chunky thighs made it challenging to walk back up to the apartment without sweating through my clothes and makeup. This led to me packing my backpack for the day when I would head out the door for yoga or breakfast. While I was at the bottom of the hill, I'd hit up a coffee shop, or go for long walks along the river, breathing the air and thinking about what comes next for this unemployed woman.

The lesson I was learning was unclear at this point, but I recognized this process was going to be far more valuable than punching a clock for some new employer. Plus, the thought of going home kind of made me feel like a little bitch. Traveling alone was empowering me. It opened me up to view myself as stronger and more independent. It was an exhilarating feeling, thinking that I might be able to do *anything*...and I didn't want that feeling to die. I couldn't leave now, I was just getting started. Besides, my reservations on Airbnb for the next several months were already booked and paid for. If I went home now, would I ever make it back to a surf village in Nicaragua? Of course not. My mind was made up, the travels would continue.

Taxi Hostage

My departure flight from Colombia was scheduled early in the morning. Since it was over a thirty-minute drive to the airport, I left my apartment one day early and spent the night at a hotel across the street from the airport. Each time I arrived in a new country, I learned how to get around in that specific place. It was never the same. Some cities had excellent public transportation. Others were so walkable that I never needed transportation. Uber existed in some locations and not in others. I'd had so many different taxi or ride-share apps on my phone that I kept having to clean out my apps because, well, OCD. Up until now, I'd pretty much walked everywhere in Medellín, so I had to download the Colombian taxi app in order to summon my ride to the hotel. As we sped up the hill, through the jungle, and out of the city, I noticed this time I wasn't as motion sick. Perhaps it helped that it was daylight, and I could see the twists and turns in the road before the vehicle yanked one way or another.

One thing I was certain I would always remember about this place was the astounding number of motorcycles. There were more motorcycles than cars, and the Colombian people were very inventive in how to travel via two wheels. As we came closer to the hotel, I even saw a man driving a motorcycle with a golden retriever in a backpack on his back. What a fucking circus that must have been, trying to get a full-size dog to fit in a backpack! Not to mention training it to hold still so you could drive a motorcycle; I wouldn't be able to hold myself upright on two wheels, much less carry a 70-pound dog on my back!

When we pulled up in front of the hotel, I instructed my app to pay via credit card, but the driver wouldn't let me out of the car. He kept motioning at the app like I needed to pay. He didn't speak any English, and we've already determined my Spanish was complete shit. It's painful. He kept saying "efectivo," so I thought my credit card wasn't be working. Efectivo must mean my card was ineffective; at least, that was my white girl in duress translation. I was feeling claustrophobic in the back seat, and I could feel my face turning red with embarrassment. My brain wasn't fully working because of the stress inching up from the pit of my stomach. I didn't have enough cash on me to pay for the ride, which created an urgency to will my credit card to work.

In the back of the taxi, with my luggage hostage in the trunk, I was frantically trying to call my credit card company to determine why they were declining the charge. The taxi driver was impatient, as he could have picked up another fare-paying rider by that point. I was gesturing wildly, trying to show him that I didn't have enough cash for the ride. As was my practice when I was moving to a new country, I spent all but a few dollars of the local currency so I didn't get raped by fees exchanging it for new currency at the airport. Now I was questioning if that was a stupid practice and would cost me becoming a taxi prisoner.

Thankfully, someone working the counter inside the hotel saw me sitting in the cab for an extraordinary amount of time, and he came outside to check to ensure everything was okay. He was multilingual and was able to translate for me - it wasn't that my card was declined; the taxi app didn't accept non-Colombian-issued cards. WTF!?! Why in the hell would the stupid app let me set up an account with that card number? Worse yet, why would it allow me to then schedule a ride? Thankfully my hotel hero offered to run my card inside for the amount needed to pay the taxi driver, and he would bring out cash. I asked him to run a little extra on the card because I wanted to tip the driver extra to compensate for the time he had to sit outside the hotel with a wildly gesturing, ill-prepared American. Had I looked up the word efectivo (meaning effective or **cash**), I would have known he was telling me to pay in Colombian Pesos. Not that I had any to pay him with, but I wouldn't have wasted time trying to call the credit card company.

It took a full thirty minutes after the incident for my heart rate to go down so that I could appreciate the nice hotel I was standing in, with a handsome bar in the lobby. The bar was empty, and it was definitely time to have a beverage and catch some rest before my early morning flight to Guatemala. As I sat down with my drink, I could finally appreciate the fiasco in the hotel driveway. Had that happened during my first couple of months in Europe, I probably would have booked a flight home. Instead, I was sitting at this bar by myself (also something I probably wouldn't have done a year ago) and looking forward to the next country on my list. If I didn't know better, I might say I was becoming confident in my travel, developing a new resilience that made me feel more empowered than I ever felt in my day to day life at home.

♥

Guatemala

Apparently, Semana Santa (Easter) is a big deal in other countries <insert dumb American valley girl accent here>. I legit did not know that this holiday was celebrated to any great extent, anywhere. Sure, we grew up celebrating Easter, which looked something like:

1. Wake up excited, time for Easter baskets full of chocolate and hunting for Easter eggs in the backyard.
2. Mom forces us to put on nice clothes and go to church for an Easter sermon.
3. Some family gathers for ham, deviled eggs, and other goodies, which slightly made up for having my hair pin-curled and sitting through a boring church service.

By the next day, we forgot all about it unless we were shoving chocolate Easter Bunny pieces into our mouths.

This was not the case in Guatemala. I had arrived in the town of Antigua one full month before Easter, yet the town was already preparing. It seemed there was a procession in the streets almost every day. These weren't willy-nilly, call up your neighbors and walk the streets. These were coordinated and prepared processions that I imagined months were spent in preparation. Early in the morning, the streets involved in the evening processions were blocked off to parking and traffic. People gathered in the middle of the closed streets with plastic buckets full of materials to build full murals on the uneven cobblestone. Literally *on* the street. They used flower petals, paint, and other basic materials to create the most un-basic-looking artistic creations I'd ever seen on a street. Not that I'd ever seen anything artistic *on* a street. Later in the day, the men of the town robe up in full purple robes, including a hood. Honestly, all I could think of when I saw the costumes were the KKK, because some of the hoods came up to a point on top. Imagine a group of purple KKK members, but they are gathering to spread love instead of hate. Most normal people would probably compare them to some type of monk, but that's not how my brain works. They walked through the streets, carrying crucifixes or large Jesus sculptures while burning copious amounts of sage and palo santo. There was one afternoon, I saw a group of these purple-cloaked strangers carrying a shrine with a giant cross, which reminded me of Noah's arc. Not because it was in the shape of a boat, but because it was the size of a parade float. But they were carrying it on their damn shoulders. At first, it was an amazing sight and I felt privileged to see such a beautiful tribute to a group of people's religion.

By now, you know I'm kind of an asshole, and I'm not particularly patient, so I quickly grew tired of the clogged streets in this tiny town. Jesus or no Jesus. If I was headed out to the market or to find a bite for dinner, it was inevitable to be held up on one of the few streets I needed to travel. It wasn't just the purple robes marching down the street, but crowds of onlookers filled every square inch of sidewalk space, and jammed between them were the salespeople, peddling water, candy, sunglasses, trinkets to keep the kids quiet, and other essentials. It was exhausting for an introvert to be surrounded by that many people all the time. Maybe I should have done better research on my destinations, but that's what happens when you buy a one-way ticket to South America and wing it the rest of the way.

Speaking of destinations, there was a reason my apartment here was only $500 for the whole month. It turned out it was the *garage* of this tiny housing unit. The rest of the complex was so cute, with a courtyard in the middle and dark, heavy, rustic wooden doors. My doors were also heavy wooden doors, but they led into a dark area that I believed was previously utilized to store tools. It was a tiny, narrow entry with a counter on the left side that had a sink and, I suppose, should be referred to as a kitchen. This was the exterior wall that ran along the sidewalk outside, and I noticed the wall and floor were not connected, there was a gap large enough to slip coins from the exterior sidewalk into my kitchen. This provided easy access for all the bugs, so my food would have to be stored in ziplock bags to avoid infestation. It was so narrow; the table was a high-top, 2-person table with a couple of uncomfortable barstools. There were no appliances, but the 'kitchen' was equipped with a small dorm room-sized fridge and a hot plate in case I decided to take up cooking. The bathroom was about the size of a broom closet, and the hot water came from an attachment screwed to the end of the shower head. Not fucking kidding. There were wires running from it, and each time I turned the metal handle to start or stop the water flow, I received a little shock of electricity. I know I make fun of all the rules in 'Merica, but I suppose there is a reason we have building codes. Each shower turned into a game of, 'Will I die of an electric shock today?' The stairs twisted unevenly up to a loft area with a queen mattress shoved in the corner under the slope of the angled roof. To say it had seen better days was an understatement. There was a visible indentation on the only side of the bed where you could crawl in or out. If I had to guess, I'd say it was at least 20 years old. I threw up in my mouth a little bit, thinking of the sheer magnitude of dead skin cells that must have been weighing this thing down. It appeared free of bed bugs, though, so I figured for 500 bucks, you get what you pay for. This was a real departure from my previous

OCD ways. But isn't 'a real departure' exactly what I'd been going for the whole time?

After a few days, I felt like I'd seen all there was to see in Antigua. It's a small flat town, and I felt like I'd walked end to end, although that certainly wasn't possible. According to Google Maps, there was a yoga studio within walking distance of my garage/apartment, but I couldn't find it to save my life. Surely if Grace had been with me, she'd have asked every stranger on the street until we found it. But alone, I shrugged my shoulders in resignation and joined a nearby weightlifting gym instead. My routine quickly became: wake up in the morning and listen to my Dr. Joe meditations, go to the gym, then go to breakfast, and spend the rest of the day trying to figure out my life. This was the most time I'd ever spent with myself, on myself. It was like the universe handed me this modest destination so I couldn't run away from the introspection and deep self-analysis I needed to do to jump-start the healing process.

Originally, I was centering my healing on my blood due to the anxiety over my bone marrow biopsy results. That was before my doctor called. When I saw I had a message from him, my chest tightened, and my mind started to race in its typical anxious fashion. What if… what if…what if. But now I was armed with all my new information on meditation, where I had learned some techniques to deal with my racing mind. To intercept my own self, I stood up straight, took a deep breath, and focused on the process of air coming in and going out. My thoughts turned to a mantra of *whatever this is, you can handle it*. My fingers stopped trembling, and I pushed the button to listen to the message.

"Nothing came back in the test results, and we will continue to monitor the situation," my doctor's voice said on the recording. Seriously? I'd waited fucking weeks stressed out about…*nothing came back, continue to monitor*. What was all the urgent bullshit about before? The warnings not to go to South America because I wouldn't be close enough to "proper" healthcare? If I had canceled my trip and then gotten those results, I probably would have at least driven by the doctor's office and egged his car. Rationally, I knew it was better than a message recommending a bone marrow transplant that I would probably refuse. My instinct told me this was not a dire, life-threatening disorder. I'd already been living with it for at least 10 years, so I was a little annoyed that I let this doc get inside my head and convince me to do this testing. All it did was bring up fear and anxiety that were a complete waste of time without even giving me a diagnosis or some way to 'treat' it. Perhaps not a complete waste, I reasoned, because would I have been as open to learning meditation and yoga if there wasn't this test result looming overhead? Maybe the fear created an opening to learn something far more therapeutic than anything I would have received in that doctor's office.

Besides, I had far more to heal than only my blood. A hematologist could only help with that *one* thing. They couldn't help me figure out my life purpose, the next steps in my career, or how to trust men. It was a gentle reminder that there was a reason for everything. I had an opportunity to focus on what I learned and gained from this situation and apply it to multiple aspects of my life. My new habits would only benefit me long term, so I chose to continue doing what I had been doing since Peru.

♥

Shaman(ess)

In researching my new hippie woo-woo alternative healing methods, I came across information on Shamans and their ancient approach to healing. Guatemala was a hotbed of alternative healers, but I was a little freaked out by some of the stories I'd read about healers taking advantage of women or having weird orgy sessions. I decided to hope for the best and booked an appointment. By luck, I found a female Shaman online listed nearby at Lake Atitlán. It wasn't too far from where I was staying in Antigua, but it did involve a fairly horrendous bus ride. If you haven't heard about the chicken buses in Central America, you need to Google it. Brightly colored and intricately painted old school buses will get you almost anywhere you need to go in this country. They are cheap but notoriously uncomfortable. While the city of Antigua is quite flat, there are several volcanoes in the area. This means my bus ride would include some mountainous terrain on roads that were not well maintained. What could probably be a two-hour drive took four on that bus. I headed on my way to a four-day excursion to Lake Atitlán; motion sickness be damned.

Once I arrived, I had to take a 'boat taxi' to the little towns that dotted the lakeside. Cars weren't allowed in the popular hippie vortex where I was going, San Marcos la Laguna. Some may picture a type of modern ferry when I say boat taxi, but I literally mean a small wooden boat with about 15 people crammed into the hull, and our bags resting on our laps for the entire ride. There wasn't enough Dramamine or sea bands to keep my motion sickness at bay during this jaunt. I was glad I booked an Airbnb for a couple of days, so I wouldn't have to make the return journey for a little while.

Little motorcycles and tuk-tuks were the only vehicles allowed in this town, so my host showed up on a small motorcycle to transport me to my lakeside apartment. My overnight bag was slightly bulky, and I was as apologetic as I could be in my broken Spanish that I was ill-prepared for this two-wheeled method of transport. With my oddly shaped bag thrown across my back, I climbed on the back of the bike and tried to keep all the weight centered so we wouldn't topple over.

I could have made the walk, but it would have been challenging to find the exact location. My apartment sat on a dirt road with easy access to the town, but I would have walked right past it without knowing it was even there. First, I had to access the lakeside through a rusty old gate which took me a few times of walking by it to remember exactly where to enter. As I walked along a winding dirt path outside the home, I was surrounded by projects at various stages of completion on the property. There was a path down to the lake with warning signs on it and a metal structure that seemed to be half-built. Even the apartment itself appeared to once have had a staircase internally leading to other floors within the home, which had since been blocked off with plywood to make a private Airbnb. It reminded me of a tree house, except this was beautifully constructed, with wood flooring and panoramic wall-to-wall glass windows on the side of the building facing the lake. Beyond the lake sat an active volcano, and I could occasionally glimpse plumes of smoke rising into the clear blue sky. It was sunny but not hot, so I was comfortable sitting on the patio overlooking the lake with the sun shining down on me. Even though there were tuk-tuks to transport visitors, I preferred to walk since I was situated close to the main paths of San Marcos la Laguna. Street vendors were selling água de coco fresh in the coconut, and I couldn't resist each time I walked by. I read somewhere that coconut pulp was used to substitute for plasma in situations where plasma wasn't available, so I'd illogically concluded that coconut water was good for my blood. A scary glimpse into how my brain makes associations.

San Marcos made the sanitation system of Peru look fancy. Back in my apartment in Miraflores, there was a trash can with a lid in each restroom which I quickly learned was for toilet paper. TP was not allowed to be flushed in the sewer systems, so it was thrown out with the garbage. But at the lake, every restroom had a sign reading,
If it's yellow, let it mellow. If it's brown, flush it down.
I thought wiping and throwing my toilet paper in the trash was gross, but the 'mellowing' process was next level. After trying to follow the rules twice in my Airbnb, I found that giant ants swarmed the toilet if I left piss 'mellowing.' There was something disturbing about lifting the lid and seeing dark blots of movement all around the inside of the bowl that was supposed to support my most valuable parts. That was enough for me, I was officially a bathroom bandit…flushing after every use. These were things I never once considered while living my stale life in the good ol' U.S. of A. Giant ants definitely kept things interesting in the restroom.

Meeting the Shaman in San Marcos turned out to be kind of like a scavenger hunt.

1. Take bus from Antigua to Panajachel.
2. Take boat ferry from Panajachel to San Marcos.
3. Walk to the tienda two blocks off the main alleyway and ask the shopkeep for directions to the Shaman's home.

4. Follow directions down a narrow path to the house with the bell hanging outside.

Shit. At home, I couldn't even find the Burger King on the corner without my navigation system barking orders at me. Just arriving at the first appointment made me feel like an accomplished badass.

I'm not sure what I expected a Shaman to be like, but this wasn't at all what I had mentally pictured. The woman was older, living in a comfortable home, but still in a very hippie-ish kind of way. We sat outside and talked for a while and then moved inside, where she made me a concoction of cacao and coconut water. She told me I should drink this every day (for no apparent reason). When she asked why I had sought her out, I told her I hadn't been able to shake the doctor's appointment I had prior to leaving for Peru. Even though I'd been diagnosed years prior with my blood disorder, this particular doctor had really gotten under my skin. As an oncology hematologist, I'm sure he was indeed doing what he was supposed to do, but it had unsettled me. Since the testing hadn't come back with a particular cause, I'd been a little obsessed with the why. Why were my platelets reproducing faster than some horny jackrabbits? I wanted a reason, an answer, a diagnostic code that I could Google "natural solutions for…" In the past few months, I had spent more time thinking about my blood than I had in the ten years prior.

"My doctor called my blood disorder a type of cancer that he didn't have an exact cause for, but I don't call it that because people associate cancer with death," I told her. "It's a fairly minor issue, and from everything I've read, I should live a long and full life. But I don't have a name for it, I don't know exactly what is causing it, and that bothers me. If I don't know its cause, how do I treat it? I came here to see if you could tell me how to treat it," I told her. She explained that I may have misunderstood what Shamans do. She couldn't diagnose or treat me, but she could help me in other ways.

Once she enlightened me on what to expect from her, I pondered what exactly I thought she was going to do and what drove me to see a Shaman. In my mind, they were like some mystical omniscient persons who could peer into my energy and body and tell me what were the root causes of all my ailments. My blood was the issue, that much I knew, but the *cause* of the problem with my blood was unknown. Since I believed that Western medicine was biased towards treating symptoms and not causes, my primary goal was to find the root cause and hopefully get a blueprint on what natural resources I could utilize to heal myself. I was already doing my meditations daily, which I found extremely cathartic. I had started taking yoga classes in Peru and had continued that until this month in Guatemala, not for lack of trying. But I had at least been going to the gym in Antigua for cardio or functional workouts. My vegetarian eating since my juice cleanse was consistent, and I had reduced my drinking down to an occasional drink or two if I happened to go out to a bar. Not that I was actually trying to be healthy on that last one. But, as a female traveling alone, I didn't think it was advisable to get shitty in a bar and walk home alone. Perhaps that was reasonable advice no matter where I was located. Besides, going to a bar alone wasn't much fun, and it seemed to signal to people that I was open to conversations that I, in fact, was not. Since I preferred not to get murdered, I chose not to go on any dating sites or accept any invitations from strangers either. Certainly I could have been more strict about my eating, but I wasn't ready to hate my life either. Just with those new habits and my pedestrian lifestyle, my ass was slowly shrinking down to a more manageable size. That had to be doing something positive for all the wonky cells floating around in my meat suit. But I was still looking for a magic bullet.

My She Shaman wasn't in the business of handing out magic bullets, only advice and sometimes cryptic recommendations. The first was suggesting I might want to stop consulting Dr. Google. Our culture was always trying to identify and name everything, there was such an emphasis placed on data and information. But if your body isn't in balance, does it truly matter if you know the name for the reason why? She went on to ask about all my doctor's appointments and testing. In the past, I'd had my bloodwork done frequently, per doctor recommendations. It would make me crazy to see my insurance being charged thousands of dollars for simple bloodwork. Recounting how one prior hematologist used scare tactics to try to keep me coming into his office for B12 shots got me all fired up and angry again. He had diagnosed me with B12 anemia and started me on shots that did nothing for my symptoms. When I told him I wasn't doing the shots anymore, he tried to fearmonger me, warning me that I could die without these shots. Side note: I bought B12 supplements at Sprouts and never had another doctor diagnose this form of anemia ever again. That's when I realized we treat doctors like gods with all the answers when they were no more than regular fucking people. Sure, they have an understanding of the systems of the body that is more sophisticated than my understanding will ever be, but they certainly aren't omniscient beings. They carry ridiculously expensive malpractice insurance because we expect them to have all the *right* answers, but not a single one does. That's impossible. So, sometimes I would have to fire my doctors. Especially when they tried to use fear as a tactic for me to comply. My point being that my relationship with the traditional health systems was already on rocky ground prior to my trip to South America.

    Perhaps taking better care of the body in general was a better use of time than seeking more information, the She Shaman suggested. It was a choice I would have to make for myself, and she made that very clear, even though I don't think you can file a malpractice case against a Shaman living on the shores of Lake Atitlán. This resonated with me so strongly. I could quit consuming information; no patch or 12-step program necessary. It wouldn't be the first time for me either. After my brother had returned from the war in Iraq and shared the way things really were over there, I realized the countless hours I'd spent watching CNN to stay informed were a gigantic waste of my time. News had been curated to make the American public feel a certain way, and I had fallen prey to their programming. Never again would I knowingly consume lies I told myself back then and quit watching all news programs. Yet, here I was, facing the same programming but related to my health care.

As humans, I think we are obsessed with both life and death. We spend most of our lives trying to prevent death, sometimes to the detriment of actually living. Yet death is the one thing…literally ONE thing, that is guaranteed to happen to each and every human. How many human hours have been spent trying to figure out all the answers to things unknown? We have no idea how big the universe is, how it is all connected, whether there is other life like ours somewhere else, why we are here, how we got here, and the list goes on. We can't handle not knowing, so we make up answers in order to feel more in control. Most people think of religion when it comes to this topic, but it also relates to health and medicine. How can any doctor have all the answers when we have no idea why the body does what it does? It is magical and self-healing, but no human could 'build' another living being. We don't have a full understanding of how our bodies operate or even how the earth itself operates. The world is still full of mystery, but we are dying for answers. We can't stand the thought that we might be nothing more than a shit in the gut of the galaxy, waiting to be birthed into another dimension.

Not wanting to stand idly by and do nothing, because I *am* human after all (or at least I think I am), I asked for some additional tangible things that might be healing for this human meat suit I was walking around in. Chakra clearing and Shamanic sweat lodging were two things that she could recommend right here in Lake Atitlán. Immediately, I agreed to everything she recommended. During the next few days of my visit, I signed up for all the things.

Chakras were something I had heard of. I knew that the symbol I so frequently saw around all my yoga and crystal shops (the one with the outline of the woman sitting, with seven colors lined up along her spine) had something to do with chakras, but I'd never spent the time to understand. I knew each color along the spine represented a chakra and that each chakra was some type of reference to energy. Apparently, the word chakra means wheel because these are "wheels of energy" within the body. It looks something like this:

Root chakra: base of spine (red)
Sacral chakra: naval region (orange)

Solar plexus chakra: belly (yellow)
Heart chakra: center of chest (pink or green)
Throat chakra: neck and shoulders (blue)
Third eye chakra: between the eyebrows (violet)
Crown chakra: top of head (purple or multi-colored)

Before we even started the real chakra work, my new Shaman friend asked me if I had been close to my grandmother, who had passed away. Super fucking weird. One, I didn't remember telling her anything about my grandmother. Two, I rarely thought about my grandmother and wasn't that troubled by her death. Three, she died 20 years ago, so what did that have anything to do with *now*? Apparently, my crown chakra, which is connected to cosmic energy and other worlds, had a deep purple energy that I was carrying around with me. Intrigued, especially because my grandmother's favorite color was purple, I asked her to tell me more. Surprised is not the right word to describe how I felt when she shared more detail, including that I needed to leave my grandmother behind. Her energy was here, but it wasn't good energy; I was not my grandmother, and I needed to let it go and relieve myself of her burden. What she said was entirely accurate.

My grandmother was a strong woman in an era where women were supposed to be submissive. She had a child early in life and ended up going through a string of men, presumably because she felt, or was told, she needed them. In fact, she did not need them (something she probably knew deep down) and seemed to always be settling for the wrong types of men. The type who leaves you high and dry with a baby, the type that gambles all your money away, the type that drinks and slaps you around - the list goes on. She predictably ended up as an alcoholic herself, becoming a shell of the vibrant woman I heard she once was. Her addiction ultimately killed her.

From the stories I'd heard about her from earlier in her life, she had worked in banking and had been the first woman to work up into higher-level positions during her banking career. Although I'd always felt an innate motivation to prove I could do anything a man could do, I didn't feel like any of that was related to my grandmother. In fact, I didn't idolize her at all. When I was a child, she had always been the alcoholic version of herself. The one that refused to quit drinking and made my mother cry with the deep sadness of knowing she was watching her mother slowly kill herself. Then, in high school, my grandmother *had* tried to kill herself. At the time, my cousin was living with her while he was finishing up high school because he was having family problems at home. Living with my grandmother was supposed to provide him with a safe space, which instead ended up with him finding her bleeding at the wrists and experiencing the trauma of calling 911, fearing she would die in his arms. It may seem uncompassionate, but I hated her for that. In my mind, it was her ultimate selfish act. After that, I wrote her off as dead to me. If she didn't want to live, didn't want to stop drinking, and wanted to be a burden on everyone around her, then I didn't want to have anything to do with her. She lived another five years after that before her body quit on her. By the time of her funeral, I felt no grief whatsoever. Just relief that my mom and her siblings could stop worrying about her.

Certainly, at the time of her attempted suicide, I had a lot of active anger towards her, but I didn't feel I carried around anything related to her after her death. I wasn't consciously trying to be her or not be her; I simply didn't think about her at all. So why was it that this Shaman had brought up the topic of my grandmother and told me to let her go? Was I internally comparing myself to her in some way? Was I feeling guilty for my anger? Or was I stuck and not processing my emotions because I'd never forgiven her for not loving herself and her family enough to pull her head out of her ass? Being raised as an instant gratification child of 1980's America, I wanted a quick answer with a 3-step solution that I could do *today*. Spoiler alert: there wasn't one.

The Shaman had done all she was going to do for me on that topic, which I guess was simply bringing awareness and making me think about it. *You need to let her go.*

Go where?

How?

What does that even mean?

These questions were unanswered, and I would continue to think about them throughout my journey.

It wouldn't be until much later, though, that I saw the parallel between my grandmother and the walls I built. I had watched her hurt her family over and over again, so I just decided not to care about her (i.e. build a wall) in order to protect my inner peace. The other significance I would unravel, after much thought, was that her life may have shaped some of my opinions about men when I was younger. Even before my awful stepdad, I knew that my grandmother had worked her way up in a 'man's world', so I always imagined myself doing the same thing. Secondarily, I also internalized that even with her professional success, she still married men who treated her and her children horribly.

Other than that, the chakra clearing was uneventful but uncomfortable as fuck. We started off sitting when she offered me a puff from her joint. My jaw was clenched, and my shoulders were squeezed so tight I think they were starting to attach to my earlobes. Was she going to touch me or do weird things to me? What dark secrets hidden in my chakras was this stranger going to find out about me? She probably took one look at my uptight, anxious stance and knew I needed to relax… immediately. It was truly ridiculous how nervous I was, especially considering all I had accomplished to be at this stage, lying on the floor in this hut to begin with. This was a far cry from the buttoned-up life of a human resources professional in the United States. But I never felt alive as that person, and now I did. So I continued as she lay crystals on all my chakras, burned some type of sage, and swung her pendulum over my chakras. She noted that my sacral chakra was blocked and suggested that I work on this area. Well, that tracked with one of my deep secrets, which, thankfully, she didn't pry about. When we experience sexual trauma, it causes the sacral chakra to become unbalanced. If I wanted to clear this blockage, I knew I would have to deal with my feelings and release them. It wasn't even that I was holding on to anger. My stepfather was long dead, and although I never 'forgave' him, I didn't think about him either. But he had been one of the defining factors forming my opinion of men and of my need for safety. The part that lingered more than any anger, was a feeling of guilt. I felt guilty that his actions had traumatized me, because I knew there were so many worse things that happened in the world. As I was feeling that guilt, I recognized the familiarity of a more recent event. Tom's actions had spurred the same feelings as my stepdad had all those years ago. The initial shock of having your world turned upside down, the realization that not all people were good no matter what face they presented to the world, and then the guilt for feeling hurt because the situation could have been worse. It was hard to admit the hurt when I felt like I had 'gotten off easy' compared to others. Like there was some limitation on how much trauma one could claim or how much healing one could receive. I was denying that I needed healing because I felt like I shouldn't *need* it. But if I kept denying where I was, how could I possibly get to the next destination?

Honestly, the entire session kind of went by in a blur, but it was uneventful in the sense that she didn't make me do anything weird. Maybe I would have to go back and try again now that I knew what to expect. As I was leaving my appointment, she offered that I could select a crystal from her collection. She had a suitcase packed full of them, and as she unrolled the various towels they were wrapped in, one fell out and rolled to my feet. A pink stone carved in the shape of a skull. Earlier that day, I had purchased a skull bracelet in one of the little hippie shops that lined the lake, so I felt connected to this piece somehow. The Shaman explained that it was made of rose quartz, so I should use this crystal to focus on my relationships and love life.

Ugh, my non-existent love life. If there was one area I needed help, my love life was absolutely it. I had come here for my health, but perhaps the guarded way I approached my relationships was a higher priority. Perhaps this was also impacting my health. The thing I was coming to understand by embracing my woo-woo was that *everything* is connected. This was definitely a sign, I decided, so I put the crystal in my pocket and thanked her for her generosity.

♥

Comfort Zones

During my previous session with the Shaman, she invited me to check out the sweat lodge sessions held at a nearby resort (I use that term, resort, a little loosely here). When I showed up the next day, I had to walk through several zig-zag outdoor pathways that led to palapas with thatched roofs. Finally, behind a handmade wooden fence, I found a large oven-looking structure. It was large enough to fit several people inside and I was immediately reminded of the childhood fairy tale about Hansel and Gretel. This large outdoor space had dirt floors and an outdoor shower fashioned in the corner. There were benches along the fence to store belongings, so I plopped my bag down and waited.

My Shaman had instructed me to bring a bathing suit if I didn't want to go in the nude. The idea that other people might be nude would typically send me running for the hills, yet here I was, ready to go into a life-size pizza oven with naked people. "Who the fuck am I right now?" I thought. When my Shaman appeared, she concluded that no others would be joining us in this session and closed the gate. A wave of relief washed over me as I felt saved from the awkwardness I imagined I would feel being surrounded by strangers.

So here I was, alone again, except for the Shaman-ess. Thankfully, she also wore a bathing suit to enter what I was now silently referring to as the 'witch's cauldron' in my mind. There was a bucket of water over coals in the corner, and that created a warm, humid environment. As I started to sweat, the Shaman handed me cacao to rub on my skin. She instructed me to rub it all over my body, and I likened myself to a Thanksgiving turkey. It was like I was buttering myself inside the oven in preparation to be eaten by some giant unknown forces. Throughout the session, I was periodically instructed to alternate rubbing different things into my skin, like honey and cacao. Inside the oven, we sweated and rubbed stuff into our open pores. Then, we left the warmth of the cauldron to rinse off with the freezing cold water at the outdoor shower.

Between the smearing and rinsing, we sat inside the oven and chanted like we were auditioning for a Native American documentary. Not saying anything in particular, the Shaman instructed me to use my voice and make whatever noise came out. This pushed me *way* outside my comfort zone even though she was the only other one present. She obviously didn't know that I rarely spoke in front of people I don't know, much less to chant, grunt, or sing. If I wasn't sweating cacao inside a cauldron, I would have gotten up and left. Instead, I chant-sung, out loud and blushed with an embarrassment only I could see.

What did I expect to feel at the end of my sweat lodge experience? Did I expect to receive a membership card into a super secret hippie woo-woo club? Whatever my expectations were, they were too high. It's like when you decide to go to the gym one time and think you will be walking out skinny after one visit. I felt like a visit to a sweat lodge would create some type of visible change in my being. But when she announced this frigid shower was our last one, and I could put my clothes back on, I was nothing more than extremely relieved. It turned out I survived and didn't actually *die* of embarrassment. Once I was dressed and had ensured all the cacao was wiped from my cracks and crevices, I decided to check out a vegan restaurant before heading back to my apartment. Even though I was slightly disheveled from all the stuff I'd had smeared and rinsed from me. I didn't know anyone here, so who cares? Besides, it was the least embarrassing thing I had done that day.

    The restaurant was nice, but it was also a reminder that Lake Atitlán was a hotbed of hippies. Whatever concerns I previously had about my appearance disappeared as I walked in and looked at the groups sitting at other tables. Mostly barefoot; some didn't appear to have showered in weeks, so if I had cacao stuck behind my left ear, no one here was probably going to notice it. I ordered a zucchini noodle pesto dish and settled in to people-watch. There was a group of young girls talking about why and how they ended up in Guatemala. One of them was saying how stressed out she was at home, and she told her parents she had to leave because it was too much. It took everything in me to not laugh out loud. Are you fucking kidding me right now? This girl was probably no more than 20 years old, and life was already that rough? Did she not learn any resilience growing up? Was her job as a barista at Starbucks while living at home with her parents paying her cell phone bill that bad? Ugh. After my sweat lodge experience, I was supposed to be more zen and less judgmental, but the whiny Gen Z gaggle made me throw up in my mouth a bit. Go out, work three jobs to put yourself through college, get pregnant and decide to keep your baby when you have no insurance, finish school, and get a job, then come back and tell me about how stressed you are. Puh-leeze! Judgmental, much?

My food came, and I was one bite in when one of the guys from the next table over got up and decided to dance around. It was like the old videos I'd seen of Woodstock, where he was dancing to a beat only he could hear, lifting his bare feet into the air and flapping his arms around, somewhat bird-like. Just when I thought I was becoming more open-minded, it snapped shut like a rubber band. *Bare feet* waving around in a place serving food? Each time he lifted his arms up, his hairy pits emanated an odor that indicated he probably hadn't showered recently. Now, my zucchini noodles tasted like armpit funk, and I'd lost my appetite. Maybe I wasn't cut out for a full transformation into hippie-dom; that was enough for me. I took my check and left.

♥

Finding Authenticity

Most people in Lake Atitlán seemed to have a lot of time on their hands. That world moved at a different pace. Restaurants would get to you when they get to you. Google Maps couldn't be entirely accurate on the location of businesses because I don't think anything had an address there. No one minded if you wandered the alleyways asking directions, though. People kept to themselves, but they were kind to strangers.

Most tourists probably tried to fill up every moment seeing the sights, there were plenty of guided activities. The tranquility of this location provided me the pace I needed to turn inward and assess my wounds and worries. It would seem I had one major wound and two primary worries. My heart needed healing, and I'd procrastinated on that task long enough. As much as I'd pushed my bone marrow biopsy to the background, there was still existing worry that was renting space in my head. Work was another one of my major worries; seeing that I was unemployed but without the constant distraction of busyness that work provided, I had the clarity to sit with myself and analyze my heart wounds. Sitting still, not physically, but metaphorically, allowed me to step through how all of my worries and wounds were connected. To heal my heart and my health would require me to shed some baggage I'd been carrying for a long time. My worry around work was also associated with baggage, the belief I had to be at a certain place in my career at this stage in life. Not only that, but I was still carrying around the emotional responsibility of the staffing firm closing its doors.

Heart, health, and career. None of these were tiny topics on their own but put them all together and it felt insurmountable to tackle them all at the same time, until I realized they are all impacted by one thing. Truth. My trouble in each of these areas was impacted by my lack of authenticity.

What the fuck does that even mean?

First, my heart wound came directly from choosing to date a sociopath. Yes, I said 'choosing.' Though I didn't know he was dishonest when we started dating, my approach to my relationships set me up for this. I'd avidly avoided truly caring about anyone (other than my family) by building massive walls around myself and not letting anyone get close enough to the 'real me' to do damage. Who did I think I was attracting with the razor wire fences and 'Keep Out!' signs? If I let anyone through the gate, it was all for show because I was still wearing bulletproof body armor.

The past couple of years, I'd been blaming my hurt and mistrust on Tom, but it actually started well before him. He was the *result* of my belief system, not the cause of it. Of course, he opened my eyes to a level of deception that I didn't realize a 'regular' person could commit themselves to. In my mind, only politicians or serial killers lived double lives of his magnitude.

Second, my health was a result of me ignoring the truth. Just because I didn't want to participate in Westernized medicine any longer, didn't mean that I had to close myself off to doing anything to help my health. Subconsciously, I had already recognized that, and it was what brought me here, to this vortex. Without realizing how it all tied together, I had already taken so many steps: a juice cleanse, yoga, meditation, and a vegetarian diet. I wasn't strict with it, but I went from eating meat multiple times a day, to eating it maybe once per month. Usually, if I restricted my eating in any way, it was strictly for vanity and was an attempt to drop weight. This time, I wasn't letting the scale dictate my behavior. Funny, it actually made it easier to follow a vegetarian diet. When you're on an eating plan for weight management, it's easy to get discouraged when you don't see progress. But when you do it because you want to, the size of jeans you wear no longer fully influences your behavior. Besides the outside influence of what I was putting in my body, I had to take responsibility for what was already taking space on the inside. In my mind, in my heart, down to the core of how I treated myself. Building walls around myself as protection, not allowing myself to feel for others, not allowing myself to feel for me...all of this manifested as disease in the body. If I was going to take care of myself, I was going to have to start living authentically.

Authenticity in my career meant coming to terms with the fact I had never intentionally chosen this career path. My plan in college had been to go to law school. After Sage was born, my goals shifted and my major was less important than graduating. There was no such thing as online school back then, so finishing my degree meant coordinating classes during the appropriate semesters, falling within times that I could attend in person. All while juggling work and the co-parenting schedule with Sage's father. There were two degree programs at my university that fit my schedule; fire science management and business management in human resources. Seeing that I was barely over 100 pounds then and probably couldn't even carry a firehouse, I had no intention of becoming a firefighter. That left me with a management degree in human resources. I was a natural in my business management courses, and the human resources material followed enough of a similar vein to law that I picked it up easily. My coursework made me *feel* successful. It's funny when you're young, there's such hopeful promise for the future. I really thought I was going to *be* someone. Each victory was celebrated and accepted as proof that I was going to be successful, whatever that meant. Back then, promoting from an hourly to a salaried employee was a major move for me; raises of 3-4% meant a couple more bucks for groceries, but I appreciated them immensely.

After years of that, I became jaded, maybe entitled even. Pay increases of 10% didn't make me happy. I was doubtful I'd ever go anywhere in this field and was questioning why I got my degree in HR anyway. My discontent eventually impacted my attitude because I felt I was destined to sit in a soul-sucking job until I could retire, which would likely make me far too old to be able to enjoy anything. Building out the staffing agency was the first role I'd been excited about in a long time, but the sting of failure made it hard to remember in the moment. Stepping down from my management role was probably the right thing for me to do, especially because without having done that, I wouldn't have been able to travel. But believing I didn't have the ability to lead the company was a cop-out. Telling myself I wasn't good enough was NOT living with authenticity.

It was time I discovered and faced my truth, and lived with it, whatever it was.

♥

Entrepreneur

Back in Antigua, I found my garage tool shop apartment even more offensive after the beautiful view of the lake and volcanos from my Airbnb in Lake Atitlán. The town was small, and I'd seen all I felt there was to see. As my restlessness grew, I decided to channel that into figuring out what to do with my life. What did I want to be when I grew up? I'd be lying if I said I answered that question in Guatemala or anywhere, but at least I devised a plan of action.

A few years back, I created an LLC for a drop-ship t-shirt company. After designing a few for myself to test out the quality, sizing, and prints, I never launched it because…I don't know; life always got in the way. There was nothing in front of me now except time, so I finished creating an online storefront, connected the drop shipper with my credit card so they could print on demand, and started designing. T-shirts with sayings like, "But first, coffee" were all the rage, but I wanted something sassier. Quickly, I became absorbed by finding sassy sayings and playing around with fonts and t-shirt styles. When I put something together that I liked, I saved it to my t-shirt shop, created social media posts, and marketed it to my friends and family on social media. It was a fun hobby, and friends started sending me requests for t-shirts they wanted printed. This didn't feel like work at all, this felt like fun.

Maybe I was inspired by all the local shops I saw selling t-shirts in Guatemala that said "Donald eres un pendejo" with a picture of Donald Trump on them. He had taken office that year, and people couldn't stop talking about whatever new insulting thing he'd done. It was funny because I'd never been asked about politics so much as I was while traveling. Everywhere I went, when people found out I was American, they asked what I thought of El Presidente Naranja (the orange president). Since I didn't follow politics or watch the news, I couldn't speak intelligently about policies or legislation, but it seemed that everyone worldwide agreed that Donald Trump was an asshole. More interestingly, it seemed that everyone in the world was following what was going on with our U.S. president.

Perhaps I was the weird one for *not* paying attention to politics. The whole concept seemed ridiculous to me. We started out as humans, all roaming around the earth just trying to stay alive. It's pretty clear that Mother Nature has control, yet some humans decided to draw a line on the earth at some point to say, "I own this." Other people listened and followed suit, apparently, because now we had maps, countries, governments, and deeds to property. Yet, when we (humans) destroy the oceans, and all human and animal life on this planet dies, a line on a map won't mean shit.

Think about it. If the human population was wiped out, except for a few toddlers, they wouldn't grow up walking the land and stepping over invisible borders thinking, 'Oh, now I'm entering Bulgaria.' I'm curious how this divisive system got started. Like, why didn't people decide the whole planet was one, and we should all be citizens of the earth, not a particular pile of dirt? Maybe that was too intangible for them at the time. Hell, they still thought the world was flat.

The fact that I think like this is probably part of what allowed me to travel alone, without interacting with anyone else except to order the occasional meal. Inside my head, there were always philosophical questions that I would never find answers to, even if I did nothing but sit alone and think for the rest of my life. It's never boring!

Disturbing? Yes, a lot of times.

Lonely? Sometimes.

Boring? Never.

T-shirt making proved to be fun, but not very profitable. My profit was about $1-2 per shirt by the time everyone took their cut; drop shipper fees, t-shirt fees, credit card fees. Once I calculated how many t-shirts I'd have to sell to stay alive, I realized this wasn't going to be anything more than a great hobby. The work I'd done in my career was very easily done on a contract basis. Even though I had mixed feelings about it after the last experience, I was good at it, and it could be lucrative if I worked for myself and kept my overhead low. Most of my career had been spent in survival mode, taking a job only to earn a paycheck, and always working for other people. On a whim, while sitting on the barstool at my tiny kitchen table in Guatemala, I created an LLC online. Not that I needed an LLC to be an independent consultant in the recruitment field, but it made me feel official and provided for a few additional protections in case something with a client went south. In a few days' time, everything was approved. I quickly self-taught on setting up a website and I was not only open for business, but I was filled with hope for the future (finally).

♥

Nicaragua

Before heading to Nicaragua, I went online to schedule my transportation arrangements from the airport to my Airbnb. One thing I had consistently read about Nicaragua was to not trust the taxi drivers. There was a company based in the U.S. that provided prearranged transportation, which I assumed would be easier because they accepted U.S. credit cards and I never knew if I'd be able to pull local currency from airport ATMs. This company was also reputable for the two-hour drive between the Managua airport and San Juan del Sur, the little beach town where I was headed. Everything was dialed in and I was feeling pretty confident by this point in my travels. I'd been on my own for a few months, and I wasn't even bored of myself yet.

The airport was swarming with taxi drivers, soliciting business with the fervor of rabid dogs. As a fairly accomplished traveler now, I knew better than to engage, so I ignored them and waited for the van I'd scheduled online. There was one very persistent taxi liaison who kept talking to me despite my resting bitch face. His English was good, so I told him I'd prearranged my travel. He confidently responded with, "They aren't coming." At first, I ignored him as a pesky salesperson who wouldn't take no for an answer. But as my wait exceeded 30 minutes, I decided to call the U.S. number for the transportation company. Unfortunately, the driver was at least 30 more minutes away due to all the Semana Santa holiday traffic. Fucking Easter was messing up my travel plans again. When I checked my supply of U.S. dollars, I counted up around $120. There wasn't a local ATM accessible for me, unless I walked back through security, so I approached the previously annoying taxi sales guy to inquire on pricing. He quoted me a price of $80 USD, so I hesitantly agreed to take one of his cars, hoping they didn't change pricing on me mid-ride.

The drive was going to take about 2 hours and 20 minutes, so I settled in with my taxi driver, who spoke a little English that was about as good as my Spanish. We took off out of the airport parking lot, and I was immediately hit with the fervor of Semana Santa. Cars were backed up for miles. Not in a first-world kind of way, either. There were a few 'regular' cars sprinkled between pickup trucks piled high with family members in the truck beds and plastic chairs strapped in front of the engine with bungee cords. There were broken-down buses creeping along at a snail's pace. But I was most surprised by entire families precariously balanced on bicycles. Literally a three-person family on one bicycle; dad was peddling, with mom on the handlebars and baby in a satchel attached to her front. Poverty in a developing nation seemed to provide a level of ingenuity that I believed 'United Statesians' were far too lazy to pursue.

After a couple of hours, I got bored of the people-watching and checked Google Maps to see how much longer it would take until I reached the sleepy surf town I was so anxious to see. Although the ride was supposed to take a little over two hours, we were only about halfway there due to the congested roadways. My driver saw me checking and explained in his limited English that, with the holiday traffic, it would probably take four hours. Fuck me. The Dramamine I took when I got on my flight hours ago had fully worn off, and I was reliant on my Sea-bands to do their job the rest of the way.

After what seemed like forever, we finally arrived in San Juan del Sur. We drove through the center of town, which was essentially a dirt road, and I saw people milling around everywhere. Along the beach, all I could see were makeshift little huts made from sticks with blankets balanced on top. The sun had gone down, so it made me wonder if people lived in them. That would suck. When I had researched the location previously, I knew the location would allow me to walk to the beach within a few minutes from my apartment, but I probably wouldn't want to do that if it were cluttered with homeless Nicaraguans.

The other challenge of relying on Google Maps was that towns like these don't necessarily have *specific addresses* for everywhere you were trying to go, so Google only got you so far. My Airbnb host had instructed me to contact her when I arrived in town, so she could provide instructions to my apartment. We were to drive to the park at the bottom of the hill, and she would take me the rest of the way. Except she didn't answer my messages on Airbnb's app or on WhatsApp. My driver pitched in and tried to call from his local phone as well. Nothing. I was starting to panic...what if the Airbnb didn't exist and this had all been a scam? Would I have to go sleep on the beach near the makeshift huts?

My driver refused to drop me in the middle of the street with my suitcases and no indication of which direction to walk. Instead, he ducked into a local hostel and spoke in rapid-fire Spanish while showing the hostel employee a picture of my apartment on Airbnb. When he came back out, he pointed up the street we were currently on, which led up a steep hill. From where we were parked, I could see the lights on inside an apartment that looked just like the one in my photos.

Thank god it worked out that I had *this* driver. If my originally scheduled transportation had shown up for me at the airport, I don't know that they would have been so diligent in helping me find my apartment. He watched my luggage while I climbed up what appeared to be handmade steps built from natural materials right on the side of the hill. These were not the perfectly measured steps we were accustomed to in developed countries. These steps were fashioned from cementing rocks together. Sometimes, they required me to lift my leg high and pull my weight up, and it occurred to me that if this location were correct, I had to repeat this journey wearing a backpack and carrying a large suitcase.

Once I crested the hill, I then had to climb the spiral staircase attached to the side of the building. The door to the apartment was open, with lights on. There was a key attached to a lanyard on the kitchen counter, along with Wi-Fi instructions. I was filled with relief, realizing that this was, in fact, my apartment. My relief dissipated as I worried about all my belongings that were still down the hill with my driver (I hoped!). I snatched the key and scurried back down the hill.

Thankfully, the driver was still there along with my stuff. Even though the trip was only $80, I tipped him the additional $40, officially wiping out my U.S. dollars. This could have easily turned out to be such a bad experience for me, but he took accountability to ensure

I arrived at my location safely, and I'd have paid more than that if my safety had been jeopardized.

The apartment was like a giant studio, with half walls separating the kitchen/living space from the bedroom and another for the bathroom. As I walked around putting things away, I noticed there were fairly large ants crawling on the wall behind the headboard. Ugh, I didn't want to have to worry about creepy crawlies in my bed. Upon inspection, the headboard was affixed to the wall but actually wasn't attached to the mattress in any way. I scooched the mattress a little further away from the headboard in case any of these ants acquired Michael Jordan's jumping skills after dark. Settled in my apartment, I started to relax and get acquainted. Normally, I'd walk around town to get acclimated, but it was late, and this little town had no street lights. There were lots of people out partying, which made me fear my sleepy little surf town wasn't going to be so sleepy. There was no air conditioning and only one fan in the apartment, so I had to open all the windows. There was a decent breeze on the hillside, which helped move some of the stale, hot air. There was also a giant mosquito net over the bed, and I wondered if I was going to regret opening the windows.

My phone vibrated, and it was the apartment host, extremely apologetic she had missed my previous messages. To be fair, she had expected me hours earlier due to the delay in traffic. It so happened she had been moving all day and her husband had packed her phone, so she had been trying to find it for hours. Even though she apologized, I was still irritated because of the frazzled introduction I received to San Juan del Sur. But after a few days of soaking up the Nicaraguan sun, I couldn't stay mad at anyone.

The crowded streets and make-shift tents on the beach disappeared after the first weekend and never returned, so it must have been just another unwanted side effect of Semana Santa. Without the tents, the beach became one of my favorite places in town. This wasn't the type of beach where I would go lay out or swim, but it was perfect for walking, sitting in the sand, or stopping for a local beer at one of the many plastic tables set out by the restaurants lining the west-facing coastline. Since the town was small, it didn't take long to make my way through all the vegetarian restaurants and select my favorites. The closest one was not the best one, but it was on my street and situated down the hill from my apartment. One day, as I choked down something raw and supposedly healthy, I noticed people walking up the stairs with their yoga mats. It turned out this mediocre restaurant was connected to a yoga studio upstairs and a wellness studio offering massages next door.

Remember the Swiss Family Robinson treehouse attraction that used to be at Disneyland? It was like a giant treehouse, and you could climb up and run around all the lookout points and wooden bridges with rope railings. That's what this yoga studio reminded me of, with its wood stairs and floor, the railing affixed with rope, and the thatched appearance of the roof above. They had a restorative yoga class that ran before sunset, which allowed just enough time to walk down to the beach post-class and watch the sun go down. As the sun slipped down beyond the horizon, it turned the entire sky bright orange, which then reflected on the water and made the whole world look like it was on fire. The beach was relatively empty, and after taking 15 minutes to walk barefoot from one end of the cove to the other, I found a restaurant offering a plastic chair and a cheap local lager.

With no work, family, friends, or plans of any kind, I merely sat and *existed*. About the third or fourth time following this ritual, I realized I'd never felt more peaceful or relaxed than I did on that beach at sunset. Like ever, in my life. There was a serenity in this town, with dirt roads and no stoplights, that I'd never felt at home. There was no rush hour commute or shopping malls encouraging you to 'keep up with the Joneses.' You could buy handmade trinkets from a pop-up table along the main street in town or stop into one of the several small shops crammed in along the uneven sidewalks.

Even though I'd been traveling for quite some time, I was starting to feel…random. There was always work keeping me on a Monday through Friday schedule, with deliverables to keep track of or an interview schedule to keep. For over a month now, I had nothing to show up for. Waking up, I had no urgent need to know whether it was a Wednesday or a Saturday. It was so freeing but also confusing. I used the time to sit inside my own head, sorting my thoughts and finally having the time to tie out my emotions to those thoughts. This was probably why I hadn't ever fully healed. As much as I thought, I didn't give myself permission to *feel something* about what I thought.

Inevitably, the negativity spiders crept in during my peace, light, and love healing sessions and started nipping at me. "Great, you're healing; gold star for you. But you should be working. How are you going to make money? You created your LLC, now get off your ass and market it. Get some business. You shouldn't be sitting here on this beach. Get off your ass and do something. You can't afford that fancy acai bowl, stop eating. Get to work. Get to work."

BUT I DIDN'T WANT TO WORK!

Steps on spider and goes back to barefoot walking on the beach.

I wanted to look at sunsets and actually see the colors. I wanted my toes to feel the sand. I wanted to wake up excited about my life again. Was that too much to ask? Why wasn't I happy making money like I was when I was 22, barely scraping by to cover diapers and formula for Sage? My career wasn't my calling back then. I was a receptionist answering the phone when I didn't even like talking to strangers! That sure as hell wasn't my calling, but I was appreciative. I received a paycheck and could buy food and gas, and that made me happy. Why wasn't I happy now that I could afford more than just food and gas? Perhaps the further away from starvation we get, the less happy we are? No. I knew plenty of people who did quite well financially and *were* happy. Everything I read said you must choose to be happy. Why was it so damn difficult for me? Why did I feel so empty and unfulfilled? Was this how I would have always felt, if I'd been able to feel, instead of being numb all the time? Maybe I should have stayed numb. This emotional shit sucked.

Instead of trying to solve all my problems, I decided to take baby steps. I learned to sit silently with my thoughts and let them pass. I learned to appreciate the vegetarian art warehouse where I could sit for hours and read or design t-shirts. I got massages. I went to yoga. I joined a gym that was nothing more than cracked concrete floors and a tin roof and focused on lifting heavy weights over and over. I took my first surf lesson because I was terrified of the ocean and decided this was the one small problem I would solve in San Juan del Sur. Not only did I learn how to stand up and ride a wave, but I was able to set aside the fact that the water was full of tiny baby jellyfish that would get caught under my surf shirt and sting my belly every time I laid on the board. I spent the month doing the little things, alone. The rest of life's enigmas would have to wait.

CHAPTER 5

Now What?

After spending months alone, with my only conversations stemming from a server asking my meal preference at a restaurant or a taxi driver asking my desired destination, I thought I might want to ease back into my 'normal' life by ending my travels with a quick vacation. Some might think I'd been on vacation the whole time, but in reality, I was just living elsewhere. Since Mexico was sandwiched right between Nicaragua and Arizona, it seemed silly not to stop on my way home. One of my favorite vacation spots is Puerto Vallarta, so I made plans to meet a few friends there. First, I took a week in Guadalajara alone, to close out this chapter. There might never be another time in my life where I spend a week all by myself (much less several months). As if to remind me how useful other people were in my life, the universe handed me a case of food poisoning. Because this leg of my trip was to be so short, I didn't stock up on groceries, and now I was too sick to get out of bed, so I didn't eat for two days.

By the time I jumped on the quick 45-minute flight over to Puerto Vallarta to merge myself back into my social network, I was feeling better and ready for a little company. I was a little nervous about sharing a hotel room after all this time alone though, especially because I was meeting up with one of my old college roommates who moved out of state, so I didn't see her that often. It turned out to be as perfect as could be; she had always been such a ray of light and still was. We quickly passed our days at the beach, eating and drinking, and even taking a surf lesson. Before I knew it, I was headed back to Phoenix just in time for summer.

Coming home was a bigger challenge than I expected. This town that had been my home for over 40 years didn't feel warm and welcome. Well, it was Phoenix in summer, so it was more than warm; it was hotter than Satan's asshole. After all the changes I experienced during the winter and spring in South and Central America, I thought returning to my little North American star on the map would feel like the embrace from an old friend. Of course, I was excited to return to family & friends after traveling alone for months. What I didn't anticipate was the daily looming of the question; NOW WHAT?

What the fuck are you doing with your life?
Are you making any valuable contribution?
If you aren't traveling, who even ARE you?

Where I was confident every day walking around foreign countries alone, I found myself insecure and vulnerable at home. What I didn't recognize was the classic withdrawal symptoms I was experiencing. Sitting still on a beach in a foreign country was more acceptable because I had no history there. At home, though, all my external cues were telling me I had to *get busy*. Isn't that what I had always done? Ignored what was going on inside by filling up with stuff on the outside to keep me moving. I was addicted to busyness, and now I was withdrawing. My ego took a major hit as I tried to assimilate myself back into our hustle culture. Realizing that I no longer fit into our egocentric, materialistic society. Not that I ever did, but I used to do a much better job at blending in. Once you are awakened, you can't go back to sleep. Which sounds great until you experience it and everything around you suddenly becomes so superficial that you start to drive yourself crazy looking for meaning in a plastic world.

Without a 'real' job, I felt like a fraud. Somewhere along the way over the past 25 years, I'd woven my identity into my career. Now that I had no title or salary, I felt naked. Struggling to find new clients or compete in a crowded marketplace of recruiters, most of whom had more resources and clarity than I did, made me feel exposed, inferior, and judged. I had ended up in a state of analysis paralysis.

I hadn't been giving it my all.

Where I usually gave 110%, I'd been holding back, relying on other people for their energy. I had been inconsistent with things that were important to me since arriving home, like meditation, yoga, and a peaceful state of mind. Letting things happen vs making things happen.

Fear. Insecurity. Anxiety.

Those old friends had entered my head and wreaked havoc with my motivation, my sleep, my energy levels, and my ability to concentrate on what genuinely mattered. With nothing left to look forward to, I found it harder to get out of bed in the morning. What was the point? I had nowhere to go. It was like all the peace I found in Nicaragua was immediately sucked out of my body upon crossing the U.S. border.

Why don't more people talk about this shit? You can be strong and scared as fuck at the same time. Success is completely arbitrary. Having imperfections doesn't make you a failure, an imposter, or any of the other idiotic narratives we tell ourselves. The point is not to *stay* stuck. You don't find yourself all at once, and the feeling of being lost is quite unsettling. We learn from an early age to mind our syllabuses and then our work calendar. We get external feedback from our teachers and bosses. Most of us were never supported in simply exploring. We had to know what we wanted to be when we grew up for dress-up day in kindergarten. By college, you sure as shit better have it figured out, or you just wasted six figures on the wrong degree.

Though my heart was restless, I wouldn't accept living in this gray area of uncertainty, so I searched for ways to get unstuck. One of the things that I stopped doing after I got home was meditating. Even though I did this religiously for months in South America, I dropped it almost as soon as I got back onto U.S. soil. So, my first step was to start forcing myself out of bed to do walking meditations around the block. At first, it was only a couple of blocks, but they progressively became longer until I was walking for the entire hour-long meditation. Sometimes, if the Phoenix sun wasn't deadly hot, I would even work up the energy to go for a hike.

Work felt like a chore that I only sporadically summoned the energy for. More often, I felt despair at the thought that *other people* make a ton of money from recruiting, and I couldn't seem to make a placement at all. How did they do it? As much as I wanted to work for myself and remain free, I wasn't valuing the promises I made to myself as much as those I made to other people. It was like I'd been lying to myself for so long I didn't even know how to hold myself accountable to *me*.

I'll start that diet tomorrow.
This is a temporary break from the gym.
I'll only have one drink.
Just take on that extra work project; it will be fine.
I'm not good at <insert thing I don't want to do>.
All lies I told to myself regularly.

Each day, I woke up without purpose, opening my eyes to the sun streaming in the windows, but with a lethargy in my body that would suggest I ran a marathon the day before. I pulled the covers over my face in an attempt to block out reality. The reality that after all the growing and learning I'd done while traveling, I still had to come home and face myself in regular, everyday life. How did I connect this enlightened solo traveler to this insecure failed solopreneur? Certainly they couldn't both exist in the same body. Both phases of me couldn't live together simultaneously. Didn't I have to choose one and live with it?

After experiencing what felt like a spiritual awakening in South America, I had expected that it should impact my life like a tsunami, washing away everything that didn't serve me. What I was not prepared for upon my return home was the way spirituality weaves its way into life, more like a gentle rain nourishing a rain forest that takes decades to grow an inch at a time. Life is more gray area than it ever is black and white. Sure, we are taught that success happens in a straight line on an upward trajectory, but most successful people will recount their path with many ups and downs. Most don't succeed on the first try. Seriously, go ask them. Maybe it was the second or seventeenth try, but most say it was the lessons they learned from failing first that made them succeed later. Why would I think I was going to be any different? Why was I so egotistical to think those statistics didn't apply to *me*, and I'd be successful immediately, with very little effort? When I thought back to times when I was happy with my work, I realized that happiness wasn't tied to the functions I was performing. I remembered being extremely happy back when I was a receptionist working my way through my final year of college. The work itself was mind-numbing and boring. Half the time I was writing papers at my desk before my evening classes. Back then, my identity wasn't tied to my title or a bar I had set for myself that I hadn't yet achieved. In reflection, I thought my happiness was due to my level of need. That job meant I could pay my bills (barely). I was grateful, even though my car had no heater, and any time I took baby Sage with me during cold morning or evening hours in the winter, it meant I had to bundle her up several blankets deep over her car seat. Instead of being angry that I couldn't afford the proper car repairs, I had a solid belief that someday my life would be different…better. There was a blind hope for the future.

That was what was missing in my soul right now. A blind hope for the future. Gratitude. A dream. Belief that there were better things around the corner for me. While gallivanting around South & Central America, I certainly had a lot of time by myself. I got to know myself better than I had before. But there was still something I hadn't fully processed. Perhaps the travel gave me permission to run away from processing my pain. But back home full-time, there was the possibility or expectation that I might meet someone; date again. With that idea looming, I had to face my biggest failure. My relationship failure. Admitting that I had dated a sociopath for five years without knowing and trying to figure out exactly how I ended up in that predicament was so painful that I would divert my feelings of failure to other things, like work. I was projecting my lack of hope for a happy relationship future onto work.

Clarity came to me like clouds blowing overhead on a spring day. Sometimes, they were puffy and full of detail, while other times, they were wispy and faint, struggling to shape themselves into anything substantial. I knew that Tom's transgressions were only possible because I had invited him into my life. The only way to move forward was to acknowledge the part I played, so I could move forward in a different direction next time. This was the only way to bring me back to a place of hope.

When I looked back on how that relationship started, I could clearly see that I never intended to date him. In fact, I wasn't attracted to him at all in the beginning. He kept asking me out, and I kept saying no. Why did I ever decide to say yes? He seemed like a nice guy, and he was persistent and friendly. Since I'm so introverted, I relied on having friendly people around me. It was a sad revelation to find that I created a five-year relationship with the man out of convenience. Since I was never really 'all in,' I didn't require a lot of things that women normally require in a relationship. I wasn't clingy, which provided him with the amount of space he needed to pull off his crazy schemes. Had I not built a giant block wall to shut out any feelings, I would have noticed his emotional blankness. He was great at pretending to have feelings superficially, but I'm certain I would have noticed the void if I had tried to connect with him on a deeper level. My comfort level was keeping everyone at arm's length, and that was how I became the perfect girlfriend for a sociopath.

The solution? Express myself. Learn how to have feelings. Not that I didn't know how to have feelings, but I needed to figure out how to identify my feelings and how to accept and relate them to other people. The walls had to come down if I ever wanted to have a real relationship, experience love, and perhaps learn to trust again.

♥

Heart vs Brain

September rolled around and I'd made no significant strides in my business all summer, so it was no surprise that when Emma reached out to me to see if I wanted to join her in Cape Town in October, I immediately said *no*.

Knee-jerk brain reaction.

Not that I didn't want to go with her, but I felt financially I couldn't. There were countless reasons why I shouldn't go. I lost my job. I started my own company. Business was slow. I had already continued my South American travels on savings. On the other hand, the depression and confusion I'd been experiencing all summer could be abated by a month if I went. That was just running from my problems again, I decided.

Until this day in September; I was participating in an online seminar by Kyle Cease. Kyle was a stand-up comic turned woo-woo guru, so of course, this combination of using humor to find yourself resonated with me. During one of his heart vs. brain meditations, this thought came to me out of nowhere:

You need to go to Cape Town

Addicted to logic and as stubborn as I was, my immediate response to my brain was, 'You're broke bitch, you aren't going anywhere except to work!' Even though Kyle had instructed us to take immediate action on whatever came up, I took no action other than telling myself to shut the fuck up…

What can I say? I'm a slow learner – sorry, Kyle!

Fast forward a week and I got another e-mail from Emma now only a few weeks before the trip. She was inviting me once again because the group she was traveling with had a couple of last-minute cancelations, and I could take a spot for a deeply discounted rate. I was mulling it over with Sage's stepmom when she said something that made my gut and brain align. She said something to the effect of Sage not remembering my financial situation in this moment, but five years from now, what Sage *would* remember was that her mom followed her heart and went to Africa. There was this feeling I got when I made up my mind about something, it's hard to explain. It's like all my normal levels of anxiety and nervous chatter melt away as a plan forms. In that moment, I was unable to ignore the signs. Coincidences aren't a thing. Everything is placed in your life for a reason, so there's no such thing as a random coincidence.

After consulting my credit card and determining I had barely enough to get to South Africa and back, I booked my flight, promising myself I'd eat light and cut corners to save money along the way. Rather than use this as another distraction to figure out my life, I decided I had to get a job, working for someone else, by the time I got back. This gave me a deadline and some direction. In order to make it different than heading back to the same old job I'd had at any point over the last 20 years, I set my search parameters for 'Director of Operations' roles. I'd run departments outside of HR, and I'd always appreciated the positions where I had the most interaction and influence within the operations team, so I determined that would give me enough variation to get things heading in a new direction.

Each time I thought about my consulting practice, I noticed myself holding my breath, too stressed or worried about failing to move, even to breathe. Paralyzed in place, not making any progress. It was as if I was drowning in the abstract awareness that I currently had no purpose. Even if I didn't want to work for someone else for the next 20 years, I had better start to commit myself to something full-time, at least to pull myself out of this phase of fear. What I was doing at that point was *not* living. Perhaps before my travel, I would have been able to gloss over that fact a little easier, but after having experienced such joy, peace, and full immersion into an action so enjoyable as traveling, I now knew what living felt like. This was a double-edged sword because I also knew that going back to work in some office, punching a clock for 'the man' wasn't going to make me fulfilled either, but it was at least action, moving me forward.

Now that I had committed to something, I could dive into the planning. No longer pulling the covers over my head in the morning, I jumped into packing for my trip and job hunting so that I wouldn't have to live off food stamps when I returned.

CHAPTER 6
The Last Act

Even before I stepped onto the jetway for the first leg of my flight to Africa, I knew this would be my last trip. Not like the last trip ever, and I was stuck in the United States for the rest of my life, but it was the last of this digital nomad experience I'd been having for the last year and a half. The big realization that I wasn't ready to work for myself was hard for me to swallow, but I'd already started searching job postings online. I'd even gone on a couple of job interviews already. This wasn't a complete abandonment of the dream; it simply wasn't the right time for me. If I were that committed to being a solopreneur, I would have made it happen already. The feeling would have been like deciding to go to Africa. Once I make up my mind, I take immediate action, and nothing can stand in my way.

Knowing this was the last trip like this made me savor all the moments. Since I didn't tell many people where I was going or even that I was leaving again, I took pictures from the airport to see if anyone could guess where I was headed. This was the longest of my trips, with about 36 hours of travel time in front of me. So, in each airport, I took long, slow walks, using the laps to try to remember the feeling. The feeling of nervous excitement, not knowing what the next place would be like, or what type of adventures I would find there. Like Christmas Eve, waiting for Santa to come, or getting on the bus for summer camp as a child, so ready to be grown up enough to leave home, but feeling so bewildered by the unfamiliar surroundings.

When I landed in Amsterdam, at the halfway point of the journey, I walked around slowly, trying to put a reason why this was my favorite airport. What made it different from any other airport? It was large, but I never felt overcrowded there, and for the most part, it was like any other airport: terminals, gift shops, food. My slow meandering ended with me in a gift shop, touching random items on the stands when I looked over and saw white socks with pink marijuana leaves printed on them. These were the same socks I bought Sage on my way home from Europe. Suddenly, I was smiling and giggling to myself, thinking of her reaction and refusal to walk around the side of the car because she thought I was giving her drugs. Why would she think that? It still didn't make sense to me, but I found myself picking up a pair of socks and bringing them to the register.

Outside the shops, I ordered a coffee and took it to a Dutch-themed teacup-shaped table to sit and wait. As I sat, I put on my new socks over my compression socks, which made my ankles look equivalent to a circus elephant, but I didn't care. It made me feel close to Sage as I embarked on the last leg of my journey.

♥

South Africa

Sometimes, the places you never think of going are the spots that make the biggest impression on you. Perhaps it is because you have no expectations, or because you are less tied to the outcome of the trip. Whatever it is, it turned out to be the case with South Africa for me. Honestly, when Emma first e-mailed me about coming with her to Cape Town, I had to look up where it was on the map. Between my ignorance and my initial inclination to turn down the trip altogether, I didn't have much in the way of expectations. The last-minute 'heart' decision to buy a plane ticket to Cape Town allowed for complete openness to experience the location through naive eyes.

The first couple of days in Cape Town, I was spending on my own because I chose to arrive before the group and get my alone time in. In order to select an Airbnb, I Googled 'best coffee shops for digital nomads.' Then, I punched their addresses into a Google map and triangulated a general neighborhood to target. Lucky for me, there was an apartment available on the same street as two of the top recommended coffee shops. The neighborhood itself didn't have great reviews due to high crime, but it was only going to be my home for 48 hours. Despite the warnings about it being dangerous, I found Cape Town to be quite safe and welcoming. Truth Coffee was across the street, and after one visit I fell in love with the local coffee, perfectly roasted with no bitterness and lattes so creamy, I could drink a hundred of them. As I sat at a long, modern, rustic picnic table inside the shop, I found myself writing blog posts with ease and losing track of time. After touring Colombia's coffee regions and drinking thousands of cups of coffee, I was surprised to find my favorite coffee here, in South Africa.

Along the streets, I could find anything from local flowers, wood carvings, or handmade jewelry along the backdrop of the old buildings erected by the Dutch and other European settlers so many years ago. They made beautiful settings for amazing restaurants, chocolate shops, and tiny bars. It was outside these shops that I was approached by a couple of kids, selling little bags full of heart stickers. The proceeds would go toward feeding the homeless. While I had never been a fan of hearts, or pink, or anything I perceived to be 'girly,' I noticed one of the bags did have a sticker of a black heart. Whenever I posted a heart on social media, I preferred the emoji of the black heart to those of other softer, feminine colors. I purchased that bag and immediately placed the black heart sticker over the Mac logo on my laptop.

When Emma arrives in a couple of days, we will be staying right outside of town in a tourist community called Camps Bay, close to the beach. So during my time in the more populated part of the city, I took time to walk slowly and absorb the vibe. To be back in a new place, in the unknown, unleashed a new freedom and lifted the fog of depression I was experiencing while I was back home for the summer. Travel felt like hope. Waking up in a new location made me feel drunk with possibility.

In what seemed like the blink of an eye, Emma messaged me on WhatsApp to let me know where to meet her. We headed off to meet a group of digital nomads we'd be sharing a house with for the next four weeks. We twisted and turned on the hilly streets leading out of the city, around an interestingly shaped mountain called Lion's Head (a local mountain that is, you guessed it, shaped like a lion's head), and back down into the high-end tourist village that was Camps Bay. It only took 15 minutes by car, but I realized my Uber rides back into town were going to need to be limited. My motion sickness couldn't handle the jaunt around Lion's Head on an everyday basis. That would be fine, except for the fact there wasn't a Truth Coffee in this more touristy area. Plus, the coworking space we had a membership at for the month was also back in Cape Town.

At first, on arrival in Camps Bay, it was a bit of a buzz kill. Not gonna lie; it had none of the vibe of Cape Town. It was…well…touristy. Full of giant homes all stacked on the hillside overlooking the ocean, converging down onto one main street running alongside the beach.

The main road was littered with convenience marts, restaurants, and tourist shops. Since I liked to live where the locals were, this location wasn't immediately appealing. It did have a beach, which was great, but October was the start of spring, and it was still pretty cold for this Arizona native. Plus, it was windy. Like really fucking windy. Since I was going to the beach, I only packed 2 pairs of jeans for the month...looked like I'd need to go shopping! Shopping wasn't in my budget, and the chilly wind was killing my beach vibe. It was enough to subdue me and make me question if I made the right decision. Was I crazy to drop everything and spend the last of my meager funds to fly halfway around the world?

My negative attitude changed when I saw the villa that Emma and I would be sharing with a few of the others. It was a plantation-style home at the base of the hill, which was older and a bit more authentic than the newer, modern luxury homes up higher on the hill. We had a cute little courtyard enclosed with a gate that must remain closed and locked at all times. This was a security measure that got drilled into our heads due to the high crime rates. One must never open the gate to strangers or leave it unlocked. There were sun chairs and a table inside the walled off yard, and it provided a stunning view of Lion's Head. We were so close to this mountain and another range called the Twelve Apostles, that great hiking trails were abundant. If I were so inclined to get a little exercise, that is.

A tiny pool sat in the corner of the courtyard, and we found out they only recently were able to fill the pool with water. The water rations were so strict here that a few weeks prior, residents weren't even allowed to water their grass or fill their pools. Showers still had to be limited to 90 seconds. 90 seconds? Fuck! I let the shower run longer than that just to warm the water up. My thick hair won't even rinse the conditioner out in less than two minutes. Plus shave my whole body? I didn't see how this was going to be possible. I guess I'd worry about that when I got to it.

Inside the house, we found charming local art everywhere. The decor was African beach house and there were bright pops of color everywhere throughout the white house. French doors opened up onto the yard, and we found there were little nooks of garden areas all around the exterior of the house. My room was one of the best surprises of the trip. I'd been assigned to a downstairs suite. My bedroom door actually led first to a hallway with my own bathroom on one side, a pantry, and a small wine bar in the hall, with the bedroom on the other side. The bedroom was large and had its own coffee maker and small table, which was a godsend for an introvert like me, who may not want to talk to people before I'd had some coffee. By far, the best feature was the French doors that opened onto the courtyard and directly provided a view of Lion's Head from my bedroom. I sighed as I plopped down onto my bed. Being in a tourist neighborhood may not be so bad after all, if I never leave my room.

From here, we were a short walk to the market or the beach, though at first I was a bit timid to walk anywhere because of all the strict warnings we had received about the crime. Everyone must keep gates locked at all times, and we had been warned not to open the gate if the bell rang without the person identifying themselves as someone we knew personally. Apparently, thieves would ring the bell, hoping you would answer, and when you opened the gate, they would come in and help themselves. We had a full-time housekeeper who was in charge of answering the gate during her working hours, as well as doing dishes and all the regular maintenance around the house. I'd never in my life seen a full-time housekeeper. Of course, I'd never lived in an estate this size either. Shit, I might never go home. Sorry, Sage!

We spent the first few days getting acclimated and meeting others in our group. The first time I left the villa, I did so slowly, checking to make sure the gate was closed behind me and wrapping my personal items close to my body, hoping nothing I had on was too flashy, attracting thieves. After a few times of making the quick walk to the market and beach, without being approached by any predators, I became more confident. There were probably thieves waiting to prey on the unsuspecting, but we didn't encounter any. The main road wound around the beach and up the hillside, and I quickly found my new coffee shop. It was no Truth Coffee, but it was cute and had great food. Each morning, I bundled up and made the 15-minute walk up the hill.

On the first Monday we were in town, our group had an intro meeting at the coworking space to get the lay of the land. We had access codes that needed to be assigned to get through their gated doorways, and our group used the time to perform some bonding exercises. As we were sitting in the orientation meeting, Emma got up to take a call. Of course, I had positioned myself sitting next to her because…strangers! Participating in exercises that required speaking in front of multiple people was also not my cup of tea. As the activities stretched on, I found it concerning that Emma hadn't returned yet. She was usually very participatory, and I knew she didn't go home because we had a walking tour of town scheduled after this meeting. She loved walking tours, and I didn't think she would ditch out on me.

As soon as our meeting broke, I wandered into the community room with a kitchen for the coworking patrons. It was there that I found Emma, sitting by herself at a table. She had a look on her face I'd never seen before, though I couldn't immediately place it. As I walked over to see if she was ready to leave, I could see that she had been crying, which was *way* out of character for this always-composed British girl. Come to find out, the call she had received was informing her of her mother's death. During our travels, she had often talked about her father, but not her mother. I knew that her parents were divorced and she was quite close to her father, but her mother was somewhat estranged from the family, and I hadn't pried for more information.

Emma's mother had been somewhat unstable for a while, and everyone in the family had tried to help and support her, but her behavior had become more and more erratic. She had been staying with some family in the UK when she decided to take her own life. Though I didn't know it at the time, Emma had always feared she would get this call. It explained a lot about why Emma was always so well-prepared, organized, detailed, and composed. She was the eldest child with a mother whose mental health didn't allow her to be present in all the ways you expected a mother to be.

It may sound strange, but the more I learned, the more I was relieved for Emma. She had carried this weight around for so long, always trying to take care of everyone else. She was only 25 years old, so the fact that this happened now still gave her a chance to unburden herself from these expectations and live her best life, just for her.

My mind flashed back to that meditation I was doing in the Kyle Cease seminar, where the thought entered my head, "Go to Cape Town." At the time, I had no idea where this thought came from, or why my subconscious would be pushing me towards South Africa. On this day, it became clear to me that there were forces at work I could not understand or explain. While I had chosen not to believe in God or organized religion, there was something out there communicating with our consciousness. That higher power knew my friend would be going through something traumatic on this trip, and it wanted me to be there. Not for my warm and cozy hugs, filled with unending sympathy and long talks full of kind words. I was still too crusty for that. But I would like to think that, in some way, it was easier for Emma to process her situation while having a familiar face in the group so that she could shed the need to keep her usual composure.

Emma worked for a consulting firm and I'd witnessed first-hand her dedication and long hours, so it was no surprise to me when they told her to take as much time off as she needed following her mother's death. But, what was shocking to me was that *they actually meant it*. In the good ol U.S. of A., you might be lucky to get a few days of bereavement since it isn't a required benefit that employers had to provide. Basically, most companies in the U.S. will knock on your hospital room door asking you when you're coming back to work. It's a complete shit show compared to how other countries treat their employees. And we wonder why obesity and chronic illness are rampant. But I digress.

Emma already had a few weeks of vacation planned after our month in Cape Town, as she had booked a safari throughout Africa. Her firm gave her the rest of the month off, prior to her vacation, guilt free. It was the most incredible thing I'd ever seen from an employer. She now had the entire month in Cape Town to simply *be*. I'd never seen Emma slow down and just exist. If she wasn't working, she was planning walking tours to learn more about our locale, or taking weekend trips to check out neighboring cities and sites. She had an unquenchable thirst for knowledge and was always moving. Now, she was still. I didn't ask how she felt about this, but as an outsider looking in, I thought it was fabulous.

The group that we were traveling with was choreographed through a different company than the one we traveled with in Europe. This one focused on 30-day trips, was much more organized, and was designed more for entrepreneurs. I definitely liked the genre of people in this group much better, as they seemed to be more mature and all on their own growth journey. It still didn't mean I made any best friends, but I didn't hate the group events. We did some group dinners and excursions planned by our local guide. She was the spunkiest person I'd ever seen. She ran a business in Cape Town teaching locals to ride motor scooters, as there was an 80% unemployment rate, and having a scooter allowed them to obtain food delivery jobs. She led several workshops for our group on topics like financial planning and identifying our strengths. For once, I happily attended.

Emma's schedule allowed me to spend more time with her than I had originally planned, but I still gave her plenty of space. She had made a couple of new friends on the trip, so she went on some excursions with them, while I stayed back to focus on my job search. It might seem unlikely to interview for jobs while halfway around the world, but I'd had plenty of experience working late into the night when I was in Europe. Back in those days, I was the one conducting the interviews, so it was actually a little easier to only have one call per night, only requiring me to talk about myself. A few late night Zoom calls later, and I had accepted a job, starting 2 days after my flight from South Africa would bring me back to the U.S. There was a bitter sweetness to it. On one hand, I knew something in me had changed, and I wondered if I could go back to being an employee for any extended period of time. However, it also provided a level of financial security, knowing I would finally be receiving regular paychecks again.

With that out of the way, it allowed me to focus on another project I wanted to accomplish before my return to the land of the red, white, and blue. Without a Truth Coffee in Camps Bay, the other cute coffee shop would have to do. Each day, I would walk the road that meandered along the ocean side, starting at the beach and steadily inclining up a small cliff with views of the endless water. Eventually, I ended up at a part of the road where the elevation was high enough that homes had been built into the side of the cliff overlooking the water. It obstructed my view of the ocean while I walked, but I could only imagine the amazing view from the expansive windows of those villas. As my view became peppered with buildings, I arrived at a little coffee shop with an outdoor patio along the road. Not one to love loud noises, I always opted to sit inside, which also ensured I'd be warm on windy days. Sometimes the short walk could be quite chilly due to the wind whipping up from the water.

Once breakfast and coffee were ordered, I put on my headphones and took out my laptop. This had become my routine each morning. The best therapy, I decided, was to write about my experience with Tom, to examine why I ended up there, and to ensure it never happened again. Not that I believed I was ready to be in a relationship again right now, but I'd already been single longer than I ever had been in my life. Accepting a job that required me to be in Phoenix full-time pretty much guaranteed that I would want to settle in and make it my home again, and I was certain that would include me dating at some point. In order to ever feel comfortable dating again, I had to go back and retrace my steps, like looking at a map. How would I ever trust that I wouldn't end up in the same place if I didn't go back and look at where I had been? If Nelson Mandela could let go of what his captors did to him, I could most certainly take control of my life and let go of my prior hurts.

As the words came off my fingertips onto the keyboard, little weights were lifted off my soul. Sometimes, I found myself holding my breath as I recounted something I hadn't thought of in a while. This was my therapy. I didn't write for anyone else to read; I wrote to tell my side of the story and to lift the tiny bags of burden off my heart.

Day after day, I wrote alone in that café. It was the single most important act of self-love I'd ever committed. With all my feelings stored in Calibri 11-point font, I learned to breathe. It was not that I magically eliminated the fear of moving forward in my life, but I was acknowledging where the fear came from. I'd given it a name and a face, which makes facing it seem somehow bearable.

♥

Epiphany

Some might say the travel was the beginning of the story, but it wasn't. It was the beginning of understanding that I had been seeking something outside myself, and now I had to turn the spotlight inward, pull out the engine, and rebuild it. It was going to be a much longer journey than those 18 months of travel. Not having a purpose was *on purpose*, to teach me to let go and be open to what happens in life, without defining the outcomes and feeling guilty about not hitting them. For 40 years, I was consumed with guilt, but I had a great life.

WTF.

Purpose is always more than what we can comprehend. Trying to comprehend is still trying to control. We want to control our lives, predict our outcomes, plan our next moves. It's the safe thing to do. Not knowing is *scary*.

I once heard our human tendency to set boundaries and develop a protective layer described as a metaphor to tree bark. Tree bark offers the tree protection from the outer world, but trees must shed it in order to continue to grow. Here is the thing, bark is continually renewed from within. As are our own self-protective measures. That's not to say we shouldn't have bark or protective layers, but we can choose how thick and crusty we want our external layer to be. Not wanting to get hurt is a common sentiment held by most humans, but some of us are more risk-averse than others. For me, my immaturity and lack of self-esteem guided my first few forays into love. Those bad decisions confirmed what I thought I already knew;

I wasn't worthy of real love and acceptance.

In order to perpetuate my beliefs, I continued to make decisions in the same way, purposely selecting men who would confirm these negative beliefs. This is not to imply that everyone I dated was complete shit. But I continued to choose men who weren't right for me, which I had never realized was a subconscious *decision* on my part. It wasn't bad luck, or a bad 'picker' as I so often claimed. It was a mix of self-sabotage and self-actualization.

Even though I had no warning signs that Tom would prey on and sexually harass young women, I *chose* to date a sociopath, which comes with risk. Yes, I just said I chose it. Had you asked me if I was dating a sociopath at the time, I would have vehemently objected. In hindsight, I was a magnet for a sociopath. After being hurt so many times, I'd completely closed myself off to feelings. Of course, I said things like "I love you," and I thought I meant them, but I was weighted down with protective armor. My life was a series of 'going through the motions.'

If you close yourself off to feeling, then you won't attract people into your life who feel.

Like Batman's Bat signal, I was beckoning a sociopath into my life. This isn't an excuse for Tom's behavior; of course, what he did was, and is, completely unacceptable. But this realization was my opportunity to release the victim mentality and take control back in my life.

Do I want to get hurt?

No.

Do I have to give others the power to hurt me?

Yes.

If I never put myself in a position to be hurt again, I'd never love, or feel, or experience the true joy of trusting someone. Over the past few years, the question, "How will I ever trust anyone again?" must have bounced around in my brain a million times. The idea of believing another man, after having the wool pulled over my eyes so successfully, felt impossible. If Tom had lied so successfully, then anyone could do it.

But there was so much evidence to the contrary. Look at all the friends I had who weren't liars or sociopaths. Or their relationships with husbands or boyfriends that weren't sociopaths. My cynicism said, "They aren't lying or cheating, *that we know of*," and I found myself more often adding conditions to statements like, he *seems* nice rather than saying he *is* nice. As if to say that everyone around me was conspiring to pull off the biggest long con of all time. I knew somewhere deep down that Tom was a one-off situation; one that I invited into my life because I was so closed off to getting hurt that I refused to honestly feel.

My path needed to change if I ever wanted to experience anything differently. At that point, my actions were screaming, "I don't want a partner. I'm fine on my own. I don't want or need love in my life. Fuck off!"

But when I was sitting at home alone in my safe space, with the armor peeled off, and I asked myself, "Do I want to have real love in my life?"

The answer was a clear yes.

I decided I did want this emotion in my life, and if that was the case, I would have to find it in myself to risk the chance of getting hurt again and allow myself to truly feel for someone else. To open my arms and invite them in, knowing they could reach around and stab me in the back, but trusting that they won't.

Hell, if they did, I would survive.

Isn't that what I proved to myself through all of this? I'm still standing and, quite frankly, in a much wiser position than had none of it happened. Had it not happened, I'd still have my heart locked in chains, circling in a loop of disappointment with no explanation or understanding of why.

My bark is shedding, making room for the growth required not only to find love from another human being at some point but also to love myself enough to let it happen.

CHAPTER 7

Afterword

Looking back now, I should have known what a process this would be. Healing couldn't happen overnight, or even over 18 months of travel. But sometimes taking the first step is easier if we don't know how large the mountain we are about to climb actually is.

It took several years of being alone to feel truly healed. Even so, once I reached that point I realized it was only the beginning. Sure, I had mastered the art of being alone, but I didn't intend to spend the rest of my life alone. So that meant I had to date. Dating was like exposure therapy. Sure, I could "heal" while not being exposed to any triggering events, but how would I handle the first time someone professed their feelings or, worse, lied to me? Dating was a truly awful process in the beginning, like a new diet. Once you get through all the sugar withdrawals and start seeing a leaner body, it's worth it, but prior to that, it just sucks. I joined and quit dating sites on multiple occasions. There were good dates and bad dates, but all of them sent my grey matter to a dark place where I imagined and expected the worst possible outcomes. It was so tempting to solve the problem by building the walls back up, but I had no intention of inviting another sociopath into my life. No, I had to do the hard work and trudge through a cornucopia of thoughts, emotions, actions and reactions before I finally felt there was hope for me. Once my mind was in a better place, I did meet someone who proved that a better existence was possible. All of this work was worth it and I was able to live in harmony while experiencing and accepting love in my life.

Dating wasn't the only thing I was re-learning. I was trying to be healthier, leaning in to all types of alternative therapies, trying out new gyms, and for a while, avoiding all Westernized forms of medical therapies. Eventually, I did go back to having my blood monitored but without any expectations for answers. Which was a good thing, because seeing new doctors didn't provide any more answers than had any previous visits. But all the old anxieties around what needed to be done for treatment or trying to 'solve' the problem were gone. I welcomed the extra platelets hitchhiking through my body and became less concerned about any diagnostic codes that did or did not appear in my medical charts. When I centered and listened to my own internal voice, I knew that I was fine and didn't need to waste time worrying about this aspect of my health.

It's almost like the changes extended to every corner of my life once I decided to take ownership of my decisions. I was experimenting with my career, which early on caused me to lose everything. Sometimes I was working for other companies, sometimes consulting, but I was always learning. Perhaps the most powerful thing I learned was that I had what it takes to rebuild myself. Once I was empowered with the knowledge that I could destroy myself financially and still bounce back, it opened a lot of doors for me. The thing that changed for me professionally was the pursuit of projects that made me happy. When I stopped chasing a title or the next step on a path I was supposed to follow, I could jump between departments, positions, or industries. Allowing myself to consult was like taking off an underwire bra and heels after a long day. Able to finally breathe and feeling less constrained by what society dictated as success, I granted myself permission to run my business and take any consulting role and work for any period of time, and the only thing that mattered was the project at hand. Ironically, what would be considered as job hopping on a resume, gave me the perspective to be successful as a consultant. Understanding Operations, HR and recruiting made me more valuable to my clients. Eventually, I did succeed in working for myself, earning more than I ever had on someone else's payroll.

There was no 21-day fix to repair over 40 years of distorted thinking. There were morning meditations, evening meditations, walking meditations. But mostly, there was a lot of failing (and still is). I failed at jobs. I failed on dates. I failed to maintain my spiritual practices all the time. I failed to *always* stay true to myself. But this is where the lesson truly lived. In learning to fail more comfortably, I learned to align with my authentic self. I had to try things and listen to my gut when it said, "Fuck no," or even when it simply said, "Meh."

As I continue to move forward, I understand my goal on this planet is to evolve. The human experience is an exceptional exercise in growth, and sometimes the lesson is no more than to be receptive to the ideas and experiences around you. The goal isn't actually the goal I set; the accomplishment, the title, the relationship, the physical condition of my meat suit. The goal is to journey through phases while learning as much as I can, acting as authentically as possible, and becoming open to the hurt of being human. Finding myself isn't an act that will ever have a conclusion, it's an experience of unlayering infinite possibilities and trusting that everything is unfolding exactly as it should be.

About the Author

An introvert posing as a writer, Christina Cridebring is native to Phoenix, Arizona, where she was born with a sassy mouth that frequently got her grounded as a child. Appropriately nick-named "Princess Thundercloud" by a particularly frustrated high school science teacher, she has been pissing people off since she was old enough to speak.

Christina has worked in Human Resources, Recruitment, and Operations but is most proud of her role as a mother and grandmother. She loves Pit Bulls more than people and rescues whenever she can.

For more information please visit:

www.christinacridebring.com